Acknowledgements

The authors and publishers would like to thank the following for permission to reproduce photographs and other material:

Aerofilms Limited (17K)
Ancient Art and Architecture Collection (8E; 21F; 21G)
Arbeia Roman Fort, South Shields (Tyne and Wear Museums) (11A; 11B; 11C)
BFI Stills, Posters and Designs (17I)
Reproduced by courtesy of the Trustees of the British Museum (5B; 12E; 19E; 20G; 23C)
Peter A. Clayton (2C; 20B (left); 23F)
Colchester Museums (20C)
Mike Corbishley (12A)
C. M. Dixon (1B; 5G; 5H; 6A; 6C; 7B; 9C; 11G; 13E; 16C; 16D; 18B; 20D; 20H; 20K. 21B; 21C; 21D; 21E; 21H)
Grosvenor Museum, Chester (11D)
Mansell Collection (9E; 9F; 13D; 17B; 17F; 18D; 19C; 20B (centre, right); 21I; 21J)
Picturepoint - London (3C; 10C; 15B; 15D; 15G)
Reading Museum and Art Gallery (19F)
Royal Commission on the Historical Monuments of England (13B)
St Albans Museums Service (17J)
Spectrum Colour Library (14B; 17A; 22D; 23E)
Turner Broadcasting (17I)
University of Newcastle upon Tyne (11J)
Roger Wood, Deal, Kent (4E)

Illustrators:

Jillian Luff of Bitmap Graphics
Paul Nicholls

Cover:

Design - Tanglewood Graphics, Broadway House, The Broadway, London SW19
Illustration - Abacus Publicity Limited

The publishers have made every effort to contact copyright holders but this has not always been possible. If any have been overlooked we will be pleased to make any necessary arrangements.

Folens books are protected by international copyright laws. All rights reserved. The copyright of all materials in this book, except where otherwise stated, remains the property of the publisher and author(s). No part of this publication may be reproduced, stored in a retrieval system, or transmitted, in any form or by any means, for whatever purpose, without the written permission of Folens Limited.

© 1991 Folens Limited, on behalf of the author.

First published 1991 by Folens Limited, Dunstable and Dublin.
Folens Limited, Albert House, Apex Business Centre, Boscombe Road, Dunstable LU5 4RL, England.

ISBN 1 85276 163 3

Printed in Singapore by Craft Print.

CONTENTS

Unit	Title	Page
1	BIRTH OF THE ROMAN EMPIRE	4
2	THE PUNIC WARS	6
3	GROWTH OF THE EMPIRE	8
4	ROMAN LAW AND CITIZENSHIP	10
5	JULIUS CAESAR	12
6	EMPEROR AUGUSTUS	16
7	CLAUDIUS	18
8	BOUDICA'S REBELLION	20
9	WOMEN IN ROMAN TIMES	24
10	HADRIAN'S WALL	28
11	A ROMAN FORT	30
12	TOWN AND COUNTRY LIFE	34
13	A ROMAN VILLA	36
14	ROMAN ENGINEERS	38
15	MEDICINE AND PUBLIC HEALTH	40
16	LIFE IN THE CITY OF ROME	42
17	LEISURE AND ENTERTAINMENT	44
18	THE FAMILY	48
19	EDUCATION	50
20	RELIGION AND CHRISTIANITY	52
21	THE ARTS	56
22	COLLAPSE OF THE EMPIRE	60
23	THE LEGACY OF ROME	62
	Index	64

1. BIRTH OF THE ROMAN EMPIRE

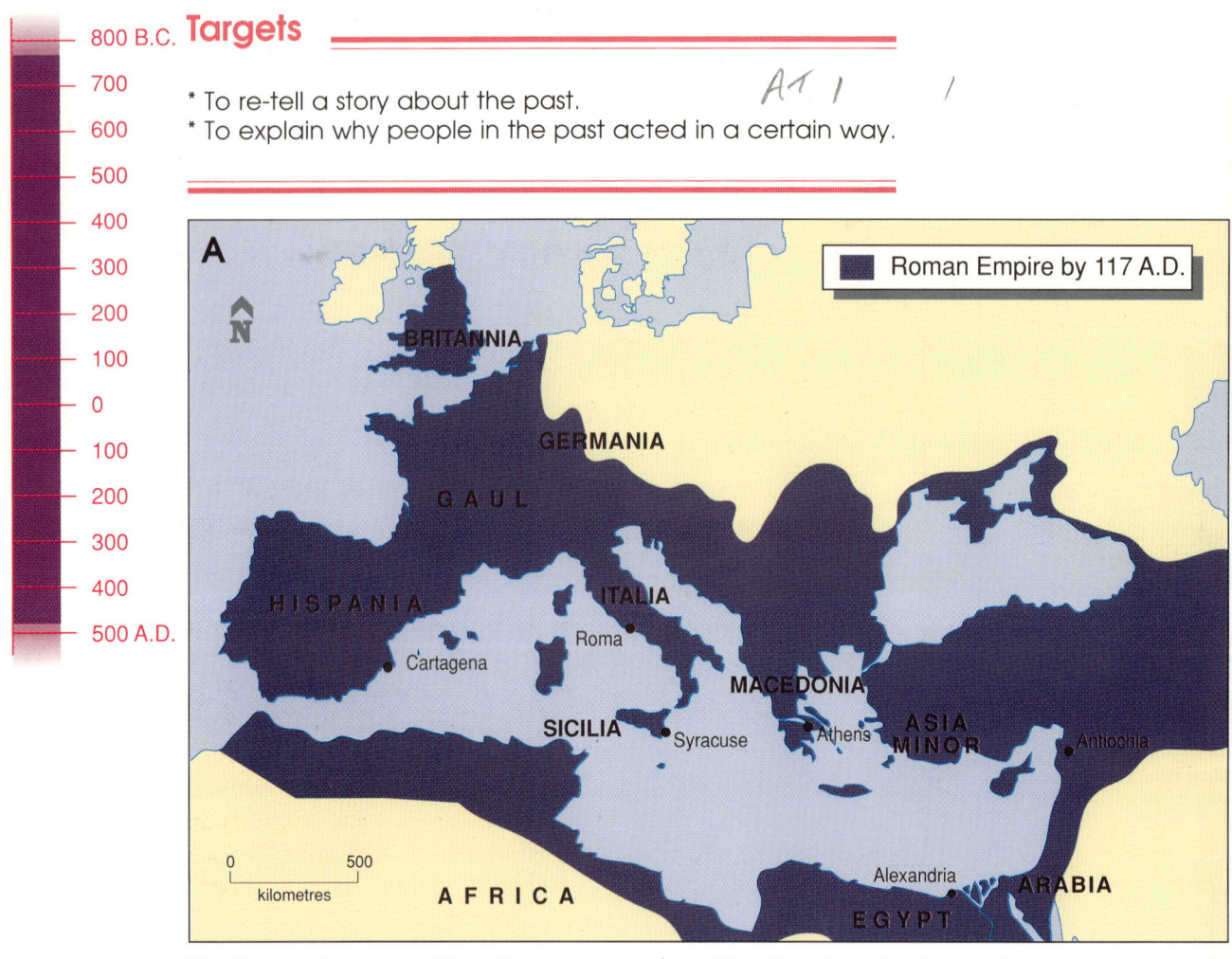

800 B.C.
700
600
500
400
300
200
100
0
100
200
300
400
500 A.D.

Targets

* To re-tell a story about the past.
* To explain why people in the past acted in a certain way.

AT 1

The Roman Empire in 117 A.D.   Was Britain in the Roman Empire in 117 A.D.?

In this book you are going to learn about the Roman Empire. The time line on this page shows the centuries covered by the Empire. As you can see, it covered a time span of over 1 000 years.

To learn about the Romans we will have to look at the evidence which they left behind - evidence such as histories, poems, plays and letters and also ARCHAEOLOGICAL evidence. Archaeological evidence is evidence which can be found above or below the ground, such as buildings, roads, statues, coins and everyday belongings.

The Beginning of Rome
In the 8th century B.C., small groups of farmers lived in villages in central Italy. In the area which is now Rome, the villages were built on 7 hills. These villages grew into one large town. The people fought many wars against other tribes. For some time the Romans were ruled by a tribe from the north of Italy called the Etruscans. In 510 B.C. they threw the Etruscans and their king, Tarquin, out of Rome and ruled themselves.

The Republic of Rome
The chief men who ruled Rome were called PATRICIANS. They were rich and powerful. Two patricians were chosen each year as leaders. The other men in Rome were called PLEBEIANS. They were poor working men who disliked the power of the patricians. In 494 B.C. the plebeians threatened to leave Rome, so the patricians gave them a small share in the government. However, it was 280 B.C. before the plebeians had equal rights.

Chronology

How Rome Was Named

The Romans had a legend to explain how their city was named. They believed that Romulus founded the city in 753 B.C. Romulus and his brother Remus were the twin sons of the war god, Mars. When the twins were babies they were taken from their mother by her uncle, King Amulius.

Amulius put the brothers into a basket and threw them into the river Tiber to die. However, the basket drifted into the shore, where the boys were found by a she-wolf. The wolf fed the babies and looked after them for some time, but then a shepherd found them. He brought them up as if they were his own sons.

Romulus and Remus grew up into strong young men. They built a town on the river Tiber next to the spot where the shepherd had found them. One day the twins had a bitter quarrel and Romulus in his anger killed Remus. Romulus then named the city Rome after his own name. The Romans said this happened in about 753 B.C.

A bronze showing Romulus and Remus feeding from the she-wolf.

CORE ACTIVITIES

1 Look at the time line on page 4.
   - Draw one like it.
   - On your time line mark the dates of the events mentioned in this unit.
   - Write a short description of the event next to the date.

2 Look at **A**.
   - What can you learn about the Roman Empire from this map? *(CLUE TO SUCCESS:* Think carefully about the size of the Empire and what the Romans would need in order to conquer and control it*)*

3 Look at **B** and read the section **How Rome Was Named**.
   - Draw a series of pictures or cartoons to re-tell the story of Romulus and Remus.

EXTENSION ACTIVITIES

1 When studying history it helps if we can understand why people behaved as they did.
   - Why do you think the plebeians threatened to leave Rome?
   - Do you think Romulus meant to kill his brother? Give reasons for your answer.

2 Using an atlas and **A**:
   - Write out the names of countries today which were part of the Empire in 117 A.D.

2. THE PUNIC WARS

Timeline: 800 B.C. – 500 A.D.

Targets

* To make deductions from historical sources. AT 3 3
* To put together information from historical sources. AT 3 4

The population of Rome grew. Many battles were fought and gradually the Romans defeated all the other towns in their area. By 266 B.C. Rome controlled almost the whole of Italy.

The Beginning of the Punic Wars

If you look at **B**, you will see that Carthage was a city in north Africa.

A

> At Carthage there was a rich trading city which traded in the western Mediterranean, including Sicily and southern Italy. Carthage's merchants clashed with those of Rome, and even sank Roman ships to stop them from trading.
>
> *From a school history book, The Greek and Roman World. Published 1983.*

? *Who does the author seem to blame for the problems between Rome and Carthage?*

The First Punic War

The word Punic is Latin for Phoenician. It is used to describe the people of Carthage because they were originally part of the Phoenician people. The people of Carthage are also called Carthaginians.

Look again at **B**. You will see that Sicily is a large island just off the toe of Italy. Carthage controlled this island. The first war began because Rome helped a town in Sicily against the Carthaginians. The Romans soon drove the Carthaginians out of Sicily, but then they also followed them to Carthage. The war went on for 24 years, when the Romans finally defeated Carthage.

Hannibal and the Second Punic War

However, the Carthaginians swore to take their revenge. In 218 B.C. their leader in Spain, who was called Hannibal, invaded Italy. He brought his army from Spain over the snow-covered Alps. Many of his men rode on elephants which were trained to carry the soldiers into battle. As they travelled, they had to build roads and bridges. Wild tribes rolled boulders down on to Hannibal as he struggled through the valleys.

50 000 men left Spain with Hannibal. By the time they reached Italy only 26 000 were left.

Although the Romans had a much larger army, Hannibal defeated them at a tremendous battle by the river Trebbia.

B

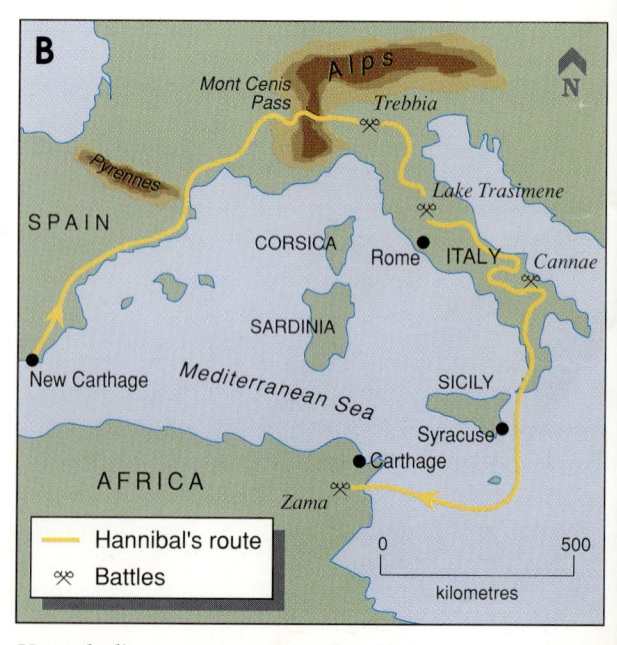

Hannibal's journey across the Alps.

Evidence

C

A Spanish coin thought to show the head of Hannibal.

? What impression of Hannibal do you get from this coin?

Hannibal defeated the Romans again at Cannae and then marched on through Italy, burning towns and crops. As the Romans could not beat Hannibal, they decided to attack Carthage. Hannibal then hurried back to Africa to defend his city. At Zama in 202 B.C. he suffered his first defeat at the hands of the Romans.

Eventually Hannibal was captured in 183 B.C. Rather than remain a prisoner he took poison and died.

D

Hannibal marched on expecting the other Italian peoples would gladly join him against Rome, but they did not. The Romans had turned them into real allies (friends). Hannibal's army was small so rather than risk an attack on Rome he marched past it to the south.

From a data book, The Ancient World. Published 1974.

? Why do you think Hannibal was expecting the other Italian people to join with him?

The Third Punic War

The people of Carthage soon built up their power again and this alarmed the Romans. In 149 B.C. the Romans attacked the city and surrounded it. After 3 years the people of Carthage surrendered. By that time three-quarters of the Carthaginians had died from starvation or disease. The Romans completely destroyed the city and sold anyone still alive into slavery.

EXTENSION ACTIVITY

1 Read this unit again.
- Then write a newspaper report about Hannibal and the second Punic war.
  (CLUES TO SUCCESS:
  - Give your newspaper a name: for example, The Roman Times
  - Describe Hannibal's journey over the Alps. **B** will help
  - You could draw a picture showing the elephants on the journey
  - One of Hannibal's soldiers might have given you an eye-witness account of the battle at Trebbia
  - You could also include a drawing of Hannibal)

CORE ACTIVITY

1 Read the statements below.
  - Carthage was a poor city.
  - Hannibal crossed the Alps with elephants.
  - Tribes along the way were friendly.
  - All Hannibal's men survived the journey.
  - Hannibal fought a battle in the city of Rome.
  - Hannibal killed himself.
- Write two headings in your exercise book: TRUE and FALSE.
- Put each of the statements into one of the lists.

3. GROWTH OF THE EMPIRE

800 B.C.
700
600
500
400
300
200
100
0
100
200
300
400
500 A.D.

Targets

* To put the growth of the Roman Empire in chronological order. AT1 i) 2
* To give reasons for the growth of the Empire. AT1 ii) 3

As the population of Rome grew larger, the Romans needed to trade with many countries for food and other goods. The Roman armies gradually began conquering other countries. These countries were known as the provinces. People in many of the provinces were given a form of Roman citizenship if they agreed to fight for Rome. In this way the Romans increased their armies and made allies (friends) of people who had been their enemies.

A

A Briton in a chariot.

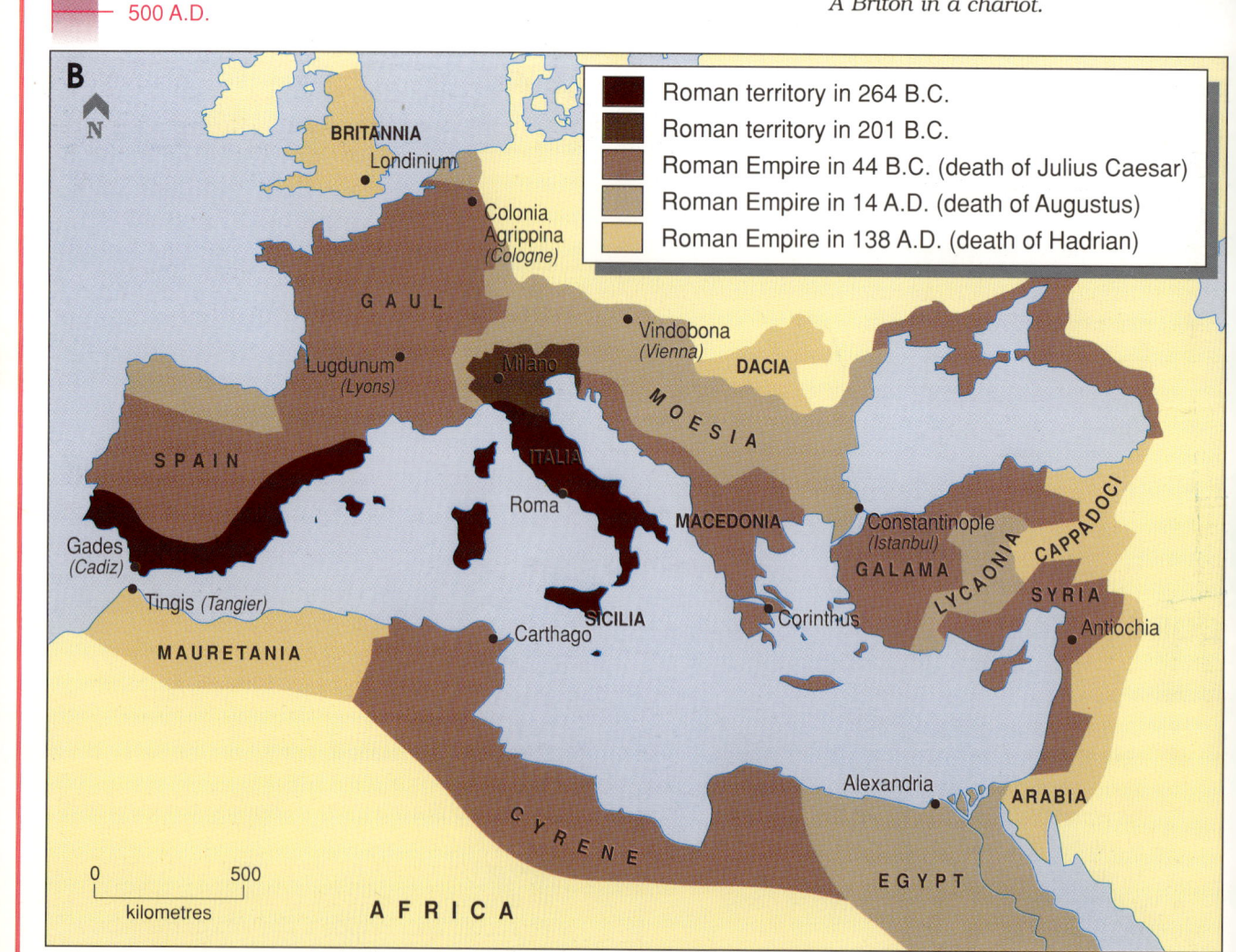

B

Map legend:
- Roman territory in 264 B.C.
- Roman territory in 201 B.C.
- Roman Empire in 44 B.C. (death of Julius Caesar)
- Roman Empire in 14 A.D. (death of Augustus)
- Roman Empire in 138 A.D. (death of Hadrian)

The growth of the Roman Empire. From this map you can see how the Roman Empire grew over a period of 400 years. Because the Empire was so large, people of many different nationalities lived in it.

Chronology and Causation

C

The Greek philosopher Socrates was one of the most important thinkers in Greece.

The Romans adopted many Greek ideas about architecture, religion, literature, art and politics. They also added their own ideas to those of the Greeks.

D

Grain, cattle, gold, silver and iron are found on the island. They are exported together with hides, slaves and excellent hunting dogs.

Strabo, a Greek writing about the Britons. He was born in 63 B.C. and died in 21 A.D. Although he visited Rome, it is unlikely that he ever visited Britannia.

? *Do you trust this evidence when Strabo had not been to Britannia?*

E

The Greeks held the geometer (a person who studied geometry) in the highest honour ... But we Romans have established ... its (geometry's) usefulness in measuring and reckoning. The Romans have always shown more wisdom than the Greeks in all their inventions or else improved what they took over from them.

Written by Cicero, a Roman writer and politician, 106-43 B.C.

? *What can you learn about Cicero's view of the Greeks from E?*

Rome imported silks and spices from the East, while from Egypt it imported corn. The Romans were also interested in Egypt's history and religion.

CORE ACTIVITIES

1 Look at **B**.
  - Make a careful copy of the key.
  - Beside each coloured time slot write the names of the countries which were conquered at that time.

2 Find a partner with whom to work. Imagine you are having a conversation in 264 B.C.
  - Explain to your friend what the benefits will be of expanding the Empire to all the countries shown on the map.
  - Share your ideas with other people in your class.

F

A Roman merchant ship used in the Mediterranean Sea. This ship was used for trade and for carrying passengers. It was 27 metres long and 8 metres wide. It could carry 200 passengers and about 250 tonnes of cargo.

? *What material do you think was used to build this ship?*

EXTENSION ACTIVITIES

1 Using any books which are available to you:
  - Make drawings or write a short description of Greek architecture (the style of the buildings).

2 Now look through this book and find some Roman buildings.
  - Can you identify any Greek ideas which the Roman builders have used?

4. ROMAN LAW AND CITIZENSHIP

800 B.C.
700
600
500
400
300
200
100
0
100
200
300
400
500 A.D.

Targets

* To identify the differences and similarities between past and present. AT 1 i) 4
* To write about information from historical sources. AT 3   3

Roman Citizenship

You will remember from Unit 1 that at first only the wealthy patricians had full rights as citizens, but that after a long struggle the plebeians (common people) were also given citizenship. These rights were not given to women (see Unit 9 for more information).

If citizens committed crimes or tried to evade paying taxes or doing their military service, then they could lose some of their rights. During the Roman Republic (509-27 B.C.) officials were elected by the people. Later, when Rome was an Empire, the Senate or the Emperor elected the officials.

Citizens' Rights

▼ To become a citizen at the age of 17 years.
▼ To vote.
▼ To hold official positions in government.
▼ To own property.
▼ To appeal to the people if charged with a crime.
▼ To become legally married.

A

2 CONSULS - Elected every year by the people. If Rome was in a state of emergency one man known as a DICTATOR could hold office for 6 months.

SENATE - About 600 men who were rather like our Parliament today. They handled foreign affairs and finance. They also discussed new laws before they were passed to the Popular Assembly.

POPULAR ASSEMBLY - This was made up of the people. They elected officials and passed or rejected laws passed to them by the Senate.

8 PRAETORS - These men were judges. They often became governors of provinces.

2 CENSORS - These made sure that citizens behaved properly. They also prepared a census of all the citizens and were responsible for taxes.

10 TRIBUNES - These protected the rights of the people.

4 AEDILES - These supervised the police, took care of the streets and public buildings, guarded against fire, controlled markets and organised games.

20 QUAESTORS - Financial officers.

Roman government.

Evidence

Roman Law and Punishment

Roman law still influences us today, because the organisation of our system of justice has come from it. Under Roman law a citizen had a right to know what charges were being brought against him. He was also given a chance to defend himself.

In court witnesses had to be people whom the judge thought would tell the truth. People could not be found guilty just because they were suspected, but only if there was evidence to prove their guilt. Slaves could be tortured to make them give evidence, although citizens were protected from torture.

B

Commands shall be just, and the citizen shall obey them ... Upon the disobedient or guilty citizen the magistrate shall use compulsion (punishment) by means of fines (a sum of money), imprisonment, or lashing, unless an equal or higher authority of the people, to which the citizen shall have the right of appeal, forbids it.

Written by Cicero, 106-43 B.C., a Roman writer and politician.

C

Those who start a riot ... are according to the nature of their rank, either crucified, thrown to wild beasts, or deported to an island.

Written by a Roman official.

? What could a citizen do if he disagreed with his punishment?

D

Those who dig up ... boundary stones, if slaves they are condemned to the mines; if humble persons to labour on public works; if of superior rank they are deprived of one third of their property and relegated to an island or driven into exile.

Written by a Roman official.

E

A mosaic showing a condemned man.

? What punishment has been given to this man?

CORE ACTIVITIES

1 Look again at the rights of Roman citizens.
- For each one explain whether our rights today are different or the same.

2 Look carefully at **B**, **C**, **D** and **E**.
- List some punishments given in Roman times.
- Which punishments do you think were given to citizens, and which to slaves?
- Explain whether or not you think these punishments were fair. Give reasons for your answer.

3 Read the section **Roman Law and Punishment**.
- Either design a diagram or write about the differences between Roman punishment and ours today.

EXTENSION ACTIVITIES

1 Using all the people in your class, make up the groups of people shown in **A**. Each group should:
- Make a large sign giving their name - such as Praetors or Censors.
- Explain what their jobs were in the government.

2 If you have time, try to find out more about Roman law and citizenship.

5. JULIUS CAESAR

800 B.C.
700
600
500
400
300
200
100
0
100
200
300
400
500 A.D.

Targets

* To raise and answer questions about Julius Caesar.
* To write two different versions of his life. AT 2

If I had asked you at the beginning of this book to name any person from Roman times, you would probably have said 'Julius Caesar'. Perhaps we remember him because he was the first Roman general to invade Britain. However, as good historians you need to find out more about him.

B

A sculpture of the head of Julius Caesar, thought to have been made during his lifetime.

? What sort of person does Caesar seem to have been?

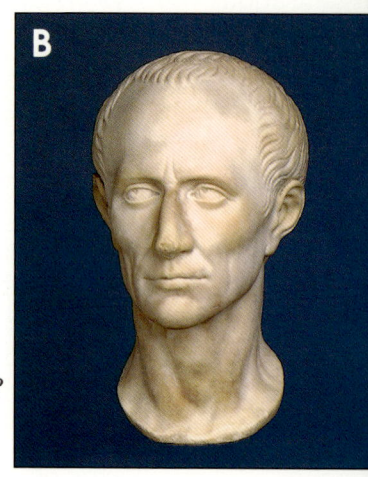

Action Slot
Find a partner and for a few minutes write down all the questions you would need to ask in order to find out more about Julius Caesar. Check your questions with the Action Slot in the Core Activities section at the end of this unit.

Caesar's Early Life
We believe that Julius Caesar was born in about 102 B.C., although he might have been born 2 or 3 years later than that. His full name was Gaius Julius Caesar. He came from a noble family, although they had lost most of their money. As a young man he served in the army.

A

At the siege of Mitylene in 80 B.C. he first distinguished himself (made himself famous) as a soldier when he saved the life of a hard pressed comrade (fellow soldier).

From a book called One Hundred Great Kings and Queens and Rulers of the World. Published 1973.

? *In your own words, explain to a partner why Caesar became famous.*

Caesar's Adventure with Pirates
While still in his twenties, Caesar went to the island of Rhodes to learn more about how to speak in public. However, he was captured by pirates, who demanded a ransom (money) before they would release him.

While Caesar waited for the ransom to be paid, he became friendly with the pirates. He told them amusing stories and joined in their fun and games. But he also told them, in a good humoured way, what he would do to them if he were to escape.

As soon as his ransom was paid and he was released, Caesar hired some ships and returned to the pirates. After a short battle he and his men captured the pirates. True to his word, Caesar put each pirate to death by crucifixion. He also got back the money paid as his ransom.

? *What can you learn about Caesar from this story?*

Caesar's Political Career
In 68 B.C. Caesar was appointed a quaestor (look back to Unit 4 to find out the meaning of quaestor). This position also gave him a seat in the Senate. Caesar quickly gained political power, spending some time as a successful Governor of Spain. When he returned to Rome in 60 B.C. he was chosen by Pompey, a famous general, to become Consul and share the government of the Empire.

Interpretation

Caesar as Governor of Gaul 58-49 B.C.
After his year as Consul, Caesar applied to be Governor of Gaul and was granted this position. Many people in Rome thought that trying to govern the difficult and dangerous area of Gaul would be the end of the ambitious Caesar, but they were very wrong.

Gaul is the area we know as France today. When Caesar became Governor the Romans only ruled the south-east corner of Gaul. By 49 B.C. Caesar had extended the province to cover the whole of modern France including Belgium and parts of the Netherlands. Caesar was able to conquer so many countries because he made sure his army was well trained. Caesar's army would follow him anywhere because he insisted on eating with them, marching with them and fighting with them.

Caesar wrote many books about his campaigns in Gaul and from these we can learn a great deal about life in the Roman army.

Caesar Invades Britain
Caesar suspected that the people of Gaul were receiving help from the Britons, so in 55 B.C. he decided to invade the island.

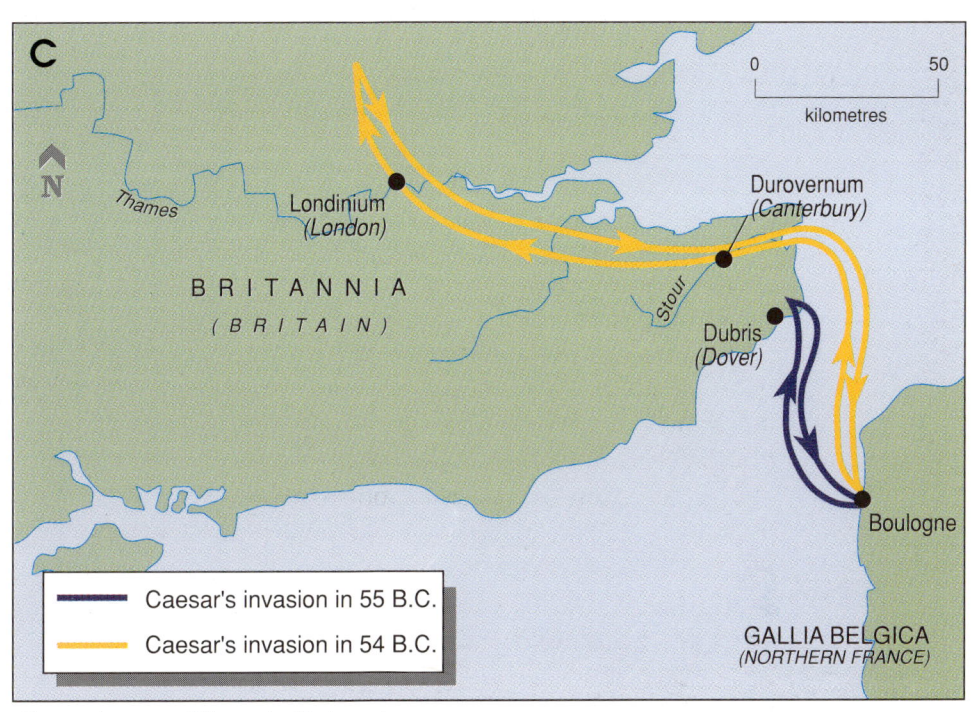

C

Caesar's expeditions to Britannia.

- Caesar's invasion in 55 B.C.
- Caesar's invasion in 54 B.C.

? What is the difference between Caesar's first invasion in 55 B.C. and his second invasion in 54 B.C.?

D

Caesar reached Britannia at about the fourth hour of the day ... he grounded the ships in a place where the shore was level and open ... but the barbarians (Britons) had realised what the Romans intended and had sent ahead their horses and charioteers ... Our men hesitated, mainly because of the deep water, but the eagle bearer of the tenth legion ... shouted, 'Jump down lads, you don't want to betray your eagle to the enemy do you?' ... Then he dived from the ship and began to carry the eagle towards the enemy. At this our men urged one another not to allow such a disgrace to take place and all leapt down from the ships together.

Julius Caesar, The Gallic War, written in about 50 B.C.

? What made Caesar's men jump from the ships and fight the Britons?

Caesar and Britannia
Although Caesar had landed in Britannia, he knew very little about the country or its people.

E

All the Britons paint themselves with a blue dye called woad; this gives them a more frightening appearance in battle. They wear their hair long and the men have moustaches. The population is very large and there are very many farmhouses similar to those the Gauls build. There are a large number of cattle. Tin is found inland and small quantities of iron near the coast. There is timber (wood) of every kind.

Julius Caesar, 55 B.C.

? Why do you think Caesar was so interested in the cattle, tin, iron and wood?

F

The fighting was fierce on both sides, but our men were in complete disorder ... they could not organise a proper attack because they were not in their usual formation. But the enemy knew where the water was shallowest. Whenever they spotted a group of our men jumping down from ... the ship and struggling along they galloped up and overpowered them, and whenever they saw a large block of Romans they drove around to their exposed side and hurled javelins at them ... Caesar ... had the rowing boats ... filled up with soldiers and sent them to help any of our men in difficulties. The moment our men got a steady foothold on dry land they made a mass charge and put the enemy to flight.

Julius Caesar, The Gallic War.

? How did the Romans finally beat the Britons?

Caesar Returns to Rome

Caesar returned to Britannia again in 54 B.C. As you will have seen from **C**, he travelled further north on this occasion. However, Caesar then had to turn his attention to Gaul, where there was further trouble.

Throughout this time there had also been trouble in Rome. There was violence in the streets and civil war seemed possible. In a bid to restore order, the Senate made Pompey the Consul. Caesar marched on Rome with his army and defeated Pompey in 48 B.C. However, there were other battles to fight in Egypt, Asia, Africa and Spain before Caesar was sure that he had the Empire under his control. Eventually he returned in triumph to Rome, and by 46 B.C. he was in total control.

Roman soldiers attacking an enemy.

? What do you notice about the way the Romans are using their shields?

Interpretation

A Roman procession of triumph.

? What do these people seem to be wearing on their heads?

Caesar's Death

Caesar was successful in restoring law and order to Rome. Many people wanted him to become King, but Caesar refused. Even so there were many Romans who thought he had too much power and they plotted to kill him.

The murder was planned to take place on the Ides of March (March 15th) 44 B.C. It is said that Caesar's wife dreamed of the plot and tried to persuade him not to go to the Senate. Even as he walked to the Senate people tried to warn him, but Caesar decided to continue. After he had taken his seat in the Senate he was stabbed by several of the plotters and died. It is said that, so furiously did they try to stab Caesar, several of them cut each other.

Caesar's Achievements

Caesar achieved many things during his life. He had beautiful buildings erected in Rome and established public libraries. He tried to help ordinary people by lowering their taxes. He also reformed the calendar. In fact the month of July is named after Julius Caesar and the calendar he devised is very similar to ours today.

CORE ACTIVITIES

Action Answer Slot
- Who was Julius Caesar?
- When was he born?
- What did he do during the early part of his life?
- Why is he so famous?
- How and why did he die?
- How do we know about Julius Caesar?

1 Using the information in this unit:
- Write out your answers to the questions above.

2 Write a short account of the life of Julius Caesar, choosing incidents from this unit which you think prove that he was a good man.
- Now write a second account, using incidents which you think prove that he was not a good man.

3 The accounts you have just written will be very one-sided. We call such accounts BIASED.
- Now find a partner and ask him or her to say:
  - which account shows that Caesar was a good man
  - which shows that he was a bad man

EXTENSION ACTIVITIES

1 Using the information in this unit, design a file on Caesar. You could include:
- his birth certificate
- an army report for his teenage years
- a ransom note from the pirates
- a map of his battle plans when he was in Gaul
- a short letter written by a soldier to his family about Caesar as a leader
- a warning note about the Ides of March
- his death certificate

2 Choose any incident in this unit and write a short television news bulletin.
- Read this to your friends and listen to their bulletins.

6. EMPEROR AUGUSTUS

Targets

* To suggest why accounts of the past might differ. AT1 AT2
* To reach a decision about Augustus which is supported by evidence. AT3

After the murder of Julius Caesar civil war broke out again in Rome. Eventually Octavian, Caesar's adopted son, beat those who had murdered Caesar. Octavian then became the first Emperor of Rome. Historians do not always agree about whether Octavian was a good man. You can reach your own decision by using the evidence in this unit.

It is very easy to get mixed up about Octavian because after he became Emperor he was called AUGUSTUS, which means 'his majesty'. Most history books refer to Octavian as Augustus.

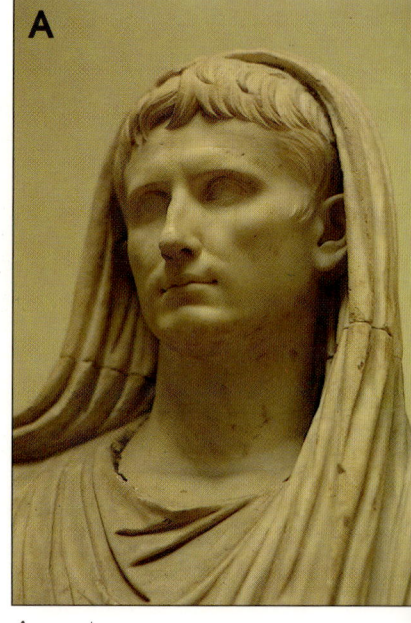

A Augustus.

? What impression does the sculptor seem to want to give of Augustus?

B

Augustus's eyes were clear and bright and he liked to believe that they shone with a sort of divine radiance (god-like brightness) ... in old age, however, his left eye had only partial vision. His teeth were small, few and decayed; his hair yellowish and rather curly; his eyebrows met above his nose ... he was, however, remarkably handsome.

Written by Suetonius, who was born in 70 A.D. Although born after Augustus' death, Suetonius had contact with people who had known Augustus.

? Are there any differences between this source and **A** and **C**?

The Early Life of Augustus

Gaius Octavian was born in 63 B.C. He was the nephew of Julius Caesar and fought in several wars with his uncle. Caesar was very impressed with Augustus and made him his heir, so at the age of 19 Augustus inherited all Caesar's money and property.

Augustus joined forces with Mark Anthony and Lepidus to avenge the murder of his uncle. In a great battle at Philippi, Augustus defeated Brutus and Cassius, two of the murderers, and returned to Rome in triumph. He became responsible for Italy, Gaul and Iberia. Mark Anthony took the eastern lands of the Empire and Lepidus took Africa. Augustus and Mark Anthony had a disagreement, and in a sea battle at Actium the ships of Augustus defeated those of Anthony.

C *A marble statue of Augustus from about 14 A.D.*

? How does this artist's impression of Augustus differ from the one in **A**?

Interpretation

What Writers Have Said About Augustus

D

Augustus called himself princeps (first citizen) but the citizens ... no longer meant anything politically ... In theory Augustus shared the government with the senate; but he governed all provinces in which units of the army were stationed, and he nominated all important officials. The senate, therefore, had no real power.

Peckett and Loehry, The Ancient World, 1974.

? *Why do you think Augustus made sure that he kept command of the army?*

CORE ACTIVITIES

1 Read **B**, **D**, **E** and **F**.
- For each source write the name of the person who wrote the source.
- Explain whether each writer is for or against Augustus and say how you know.
- You could try to explain why some of these writers hold their particular view of Augustus.

2 Make two columns in your exercise book.
- At the top of one column write 'Good Points'. At the top of the other write 'Bad Points'.
- Using all the information in this unit, write all the good points about Augustus in one column and all the bad points in the other.
- Now try to decide which of these phrases best describes Augustus:
  - He was a good Emperor who wanted to make the Empire peaceful.
  - He was a cruel, vain man who lived a luxurious life.
  - He did many good things for the Empire, although sometimes he had to be cruel to keep the peace.
- Write down the phrase you have chosen and try to use some evidence from this unit to support your choice. For example, you might put: *'I think the second phrase describes Augustus because in source E it says, 'Augustus put to death Caesarion ...'.'*

3 With a partner talk about the decision you have made.
- Do you agree with each other?

E

After this battle (Actium) Anthony sued (asked) for peace, but Augustus ordered him to commit suicide and satisfied himself that he had been obeyed by inspecting the corpse (Anthony's dead body) ... Augustus put to death Caesarion, the son of Cleopatra and Julius Caesar, as well as Mark Anthony's son by his own sister Fulvia. (Fulvia was the sister of Augustus - so Augustus put to death his own nephew.)

Edward Ashcroft, an historian, 1973.

F

Augustus made peace and security possible ... Augustus tried his best, despite poor health, to rise to his responsibilities. He worked hard, travelled widely, cautiously strengthened and extended the empire, and selected with care the hundreds of men on whom he had to rely for the day-to-day administration of the armies and the civil government. He provided an example of plain, sober living in his efforts to restrain luxury.

Peckett and Loehry, The Ancient World, 1974.

The Death of Augustus

Augustus became ill while travelling in southern Italy. He died in his father's house on the 19th August (the month is named after him) 14 A.D. A month after his death the Senate made him a god.

Augustus' main achievement was that he brought a period of peace and stability to the Roman Empire which lasted almost 200 years.

EXTENSION ACTIVITY

1 Using the information in this unit:
- Write a short account of your life as if you are Augustus. If you wish, you could do this as a comic strip or a cartoon.

7. CLAUDIUS

Target

* To use historical sources to answer questions about the past.

A1 3

During the hundred years which followed the invasions of Julius Caesar, many Roman trading ships came to the shores of Britannia bringing silver goods, cloth and wine in exchange for leather, wool, lead and tin. Some of the richer chiefs in the south-east of Britannia began to live in the Roman style.

In Rome, Claudius became Emperor in 41 A.D., but he did not have as much support from the Roman citizens as he wanted. He worried that the army might not remain loyal to him. A successful battle was needed, with plenty of booty for the soldiers! Claudius decided to invade Britannia and placed Aulus Plautius in command of the expedition.

A

Plautius split his men into three groups to cross the straits (sea). This was to make sure they were not all prevented from landing ... but there was no one waiting to meet them. The Britons had received wrong information and were not expecting them!

Dio Cassius, a Greek historian who wrote a history of Rome in 229 A.D., based on accounts from the time.

? Dio Cassius wrote his book more than 150 years after the invasion. Is this still useful evidence? Give reasons for your answer.

Some of the tribes in the south-east surrendered and made peace with the Romans, but other tribes prepared for war. Two of the chieftains, Togodumnus and Caratacus, who were brothers, joined forces to fight. They had a battle with the Romans beside the river Medway.

A battle scene.

? Can you spot which are the Roman soldiers?

Evidence

In the battle Togodumnus was killed, but Caratacus escaped. Plautius marched on to the Thames after sending a messenger to Rome. Then he waited for the arrival of Emperor Claudius.

C

In fact Claudius was ready waiting to come with a large army, well equipped with armaments including elephants ... he reached Oceanus and crossed over to Britannia and joined the legions that were waiting for him on the Taesis (Thames). Then he attacked the barbarians who had come together to meet him as he advanced. He defeated them in battle and captured Camulodunum (Colchester), the capital of Cunobelin.

Dio Cassius, 229 A.D.

D

A Roman catapult for throwing boulders.

? *Explain to a friend how this catapult might have worked.*

CORE ACTIVITIES

1 Look back at this unit.
- Why do you think Claudius wanted to invade Britain?

2 Look at **B**.
- Draw a sketch to show how a Roman soldier dressed.
- What sort of weapons are the Romans using?
- Are the Romans winning or losing?

3 Read **C**.
- Is there anything surprising about what Claudius brought to Britain?

4 Look at **G** in Unit 5.
- Explain what you think a tortoiseshell formation might have been.

? *Why do you think Plautius sent for Claudius to come to Britain?*

Claudius stayed in Britain for only two weeks. On leaving, he told Plautius 'to conquer the rest'. When Claudius arrived back in Rome he was given the title 'Britannicus' by the Senate, and a festival was held every year to celebrate his great victory.

During the invasion many of the Britons' hillforts were captured. The Romans used a type of huge catapult to fire arrows and large stones into the forts.

E

The Romans pushed forward to the parapets. The struggle there was fierce. The Romans advanced under a tortoiseshell formation of shields and broke through the enemy's wall ... The Britons, without breastplates and helmets, could not hold out. The legionaries, with swords or javelins (spears), carried all before them. The auxiliaries, with spears and swords, slaughtered the enemy.

Tacitus, 57-117 A.D.

? *Why do you think the Britons lost this battle?*

After their first successes the Romans began turning southern Britain into a province of Rome. The land was settled by veteran (older) Roman soldiers, helped by friendly chiefs of the tribes. Any further resistance to Roman rule was dealt with very ruthlessly, and by 61 A.D. the southern area of Britain was peaceful.

EXTENSION ACTIVITY

1 Using any books which are available to you:
- Find out more about Caratacus.
- You could work with some of your friends and prepare a short play about the life of Caratacus.

8. BOUDICA'S REBELLION

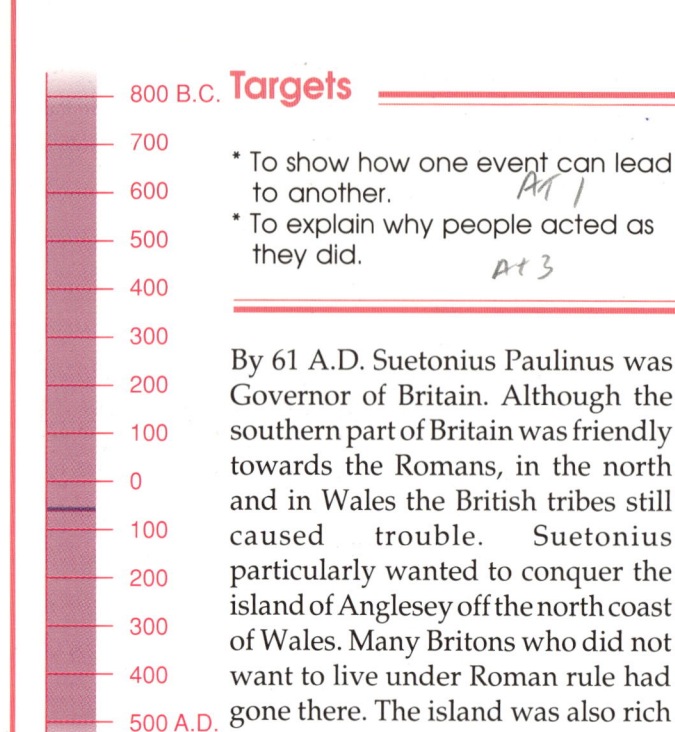

Targets

* To show how one event can lead to another. *At 1*
* To explain why people acted as they did. *At 3*

By 61 A.D. Suetonius Paulinus was Governor of Britain. Although the southern part of Britain was friendly towards the Romans, in the north and in Wales the British tribes still caused trouble. Suetonius particularly wanted to conquer the island of Anglesey off the north coast of Wales. Many Britons who did not want to live under Roman rule had gone there. The island was also rich in copper and corn.

Suetonius had another reason, too. The chief priests of the British tribes lived on Anglesey. They were called Druids and they often advised the leaders of the Britons to attack the Romans.

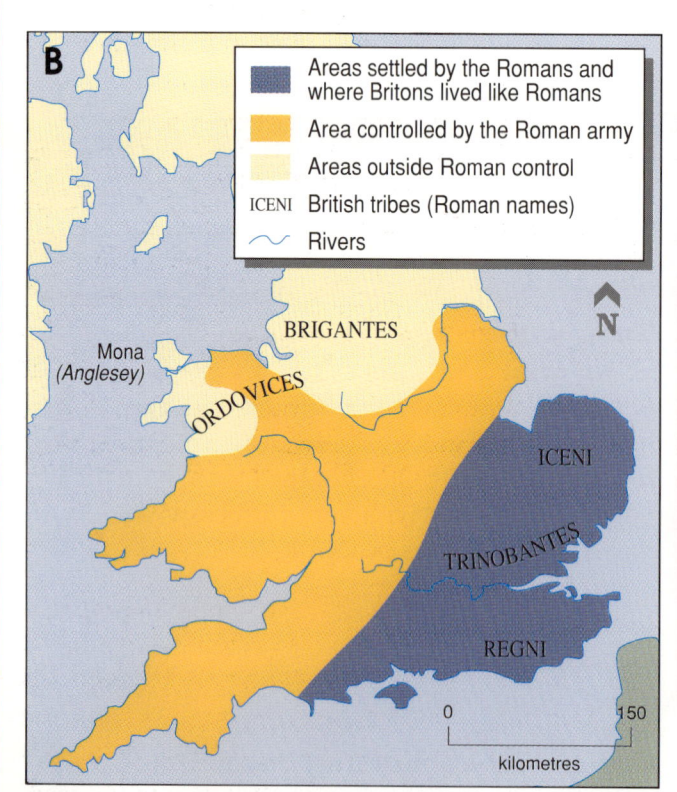

Britain at the time of Boudica's rebellion.

A

The Druids' job is to perform sacrifices, worship the gods and interpret (explain) religious matters. They act as judges in all public and private disputes ... They decide what rewards and punishments are to be given out ... Their main teaching is that souls do not die but when a man dies his soul passes to someone else. This belief helps to make them brave ... In addition, they are always discussing such matters as the stars and their movements, the size of the universe and the earth, the nature of the universe and the power of the immortal gods. And they pass on this learning to the younger generation.

Julius Caesar, The Gallic War, written in about 50 B.C.

? Why do you think Suetonius wanted to conquer the Druids?

C

He (Suetonius) planned an attack on Mona (Anglesey). Before them on the shore stood the enemy ... bristling with weapons ... a circle of Druids ... screamed out terrible curses ... Then they (the Romans) charged forward behind their standards ... They hacked down anyone who tried to stop them ... The next step was to station a garrison among the conquered population and to destroy the groves (woods) which were dedicated to their savage and superstitious practices. For it is part of their religion to soak their altars with the blood of their prisoners and to consult their gods by inspecting human entrails (guts).

Cornelius Tacitus, The Annals, written in about the 1st century A.D.

? What do you think Tacitus means by 'their savage and superstitious practices'?

Causation and Motivation

The Rebellion

After the battle against the Druids, Suetonius received news of a rebellion in southern Britain. Prasutagus, who was King of the Iceni tribe and friendly towards the Romans, had died. He had been a very wealthy man and he wanted to be sure that after his death his family and kingdom would be safe. So Prasutagus left half his wealth to his two daughters and the other half to the Roman Emperor, Nero. The Roman writer Tacitus tells us how the plan of Prasutagus went wrong.

D

He did this thinking that it would mean that his kingdom and his family would be safe when he died. What happened was quite the opposite, for his kingdom was ravaged by centurions (Roman soldiers) and his house by slaves ... Boudica (the wife of Prasutagus) was flogged and her daughters were raped ... All the chief men of the Iceni had their farms taken away from them and the King's own family were treated like slaves. Infuriated by these outrages and by the fear of worse to come they urged the Trinobantes to join with them along with other tribes.

Cornelius Tacitus, The Annals.

? *What do you think made the Roman soldiers attack the family of Prasutagus?*

E

A Victorian statue of Boudica, on the Victoria Embankment, London.

This statue was made 1 800 years after Boudica's death. Do you think it is still useful historical evidence?

Boudica's Revenge

As you can imagine, Boudica and all the Iceni tribe were determined to seek their revenge for the treatment they had received from the Romans. Several other tribes joined them at Colchester.

F

They (the Britons) particularly hated the Roman veterans (retired soldiers) who had recently settled at Camulodunum (Colchester). These veterans had ... driven people from their own lands.

Cornelius Tacitus, The Annals.

? *Why did the Britons hate the Roman veterans?*

The Roman veterans also built a temple to Emperor Claudius at Colchester and expected the Britons to give money towards the building and to worship the Emperor. Boudica gathered together a huge army and marched against Colchester. Although the Romans sent for help, the nearest legions were more than 160 kilometres away.

G

They (the Romans) were encircled by a large crowd of barbarians (Britons). Everything was ransacked or set on fire during the first attack. Only the temple ... managed to hold out in a two-day siege, before it too was overthrown.

Cornelius Tacitus, The Annals.

? *Which side do you think Tacitus is on? Give reasons for your answer.*

Boudica and the tribes who joined her killed all the Romans at Colchester and then went on to fight against the 9th Legion, which had hurried south from Lincoln. You can see the legion's route in **H**. The Britons drove the cavalry of the 9th Legion back to Lincoln and killed all the foot soldiers.

H

Map legend:
- Boudica's army
- 14th and 20th Roman Legion
- 9th Roman Legion
- ✂ Battle

Locations shown: Mona (Anglesey), Deva (Chester), Viroconium (Wroxeter), Glevum (Gloucester), Verulamium (St Albans), Londinium (London), Camulodunum (Colchester), Lindum (Lincoln).

- Suetonius' 14th and 20th Legions
- 9th Legion
- Boudica's army
- 2nd Legion refused to move

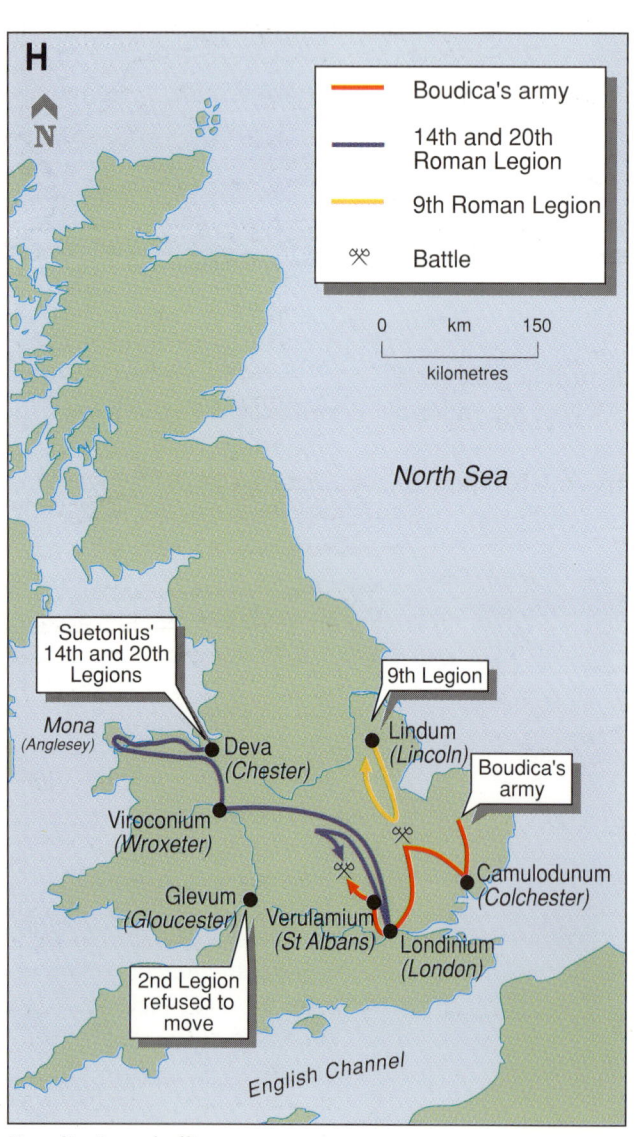

Boudica's rebellion.

I

The rebels considered Boudica to be their ablest leader ... She was very tall, and she looked terrifying with a fierce glint in her eyes and with a raucous (loud) voice. A great mass of startling yellow hair hung down to her hips. Around her neck she had a huge torque (a heavy, choker-type necklace) of gold and she wore a dress of many colours with a thin cloak over it pinned together with a brooch. She had gathered together an army of about 120 000 men.

Dio Cassius, a Greek historian, 229 A.D.

? *Using **I**, describe Boudica to a friend. Say what sort of person you think she might have been.*

The Battle

Meanwhile Suetonius marched from Wales to Londinium (London) to face Boudica. When he arrived in Londinium and heard about the size of Boudica's army, he realised that he would need more troops so he turned northwards again.

Boudica arrived at Londinium and burnt it to the ground, killing some 70 000 Roman citizens who were still there. Even today workmen often find the ashes of the Roman buildings some 3 metres below the London streets.

Suetonius gathered together more Roman troops and prepared for battle.

Causation and Motivation

J

Suetonius chose a site which was approached by a narrow valley and which was hemmed in at the far end by a wood. He sent out scouts to make sure there were no enemy in the rear and to check that there was nowhere on the plain before him where they could set up an ambush. He ordered his legionaries to bunch up in close formation and surrounded them with troops. On the wing he massed the cavalry.

The Britons, on the other hand, dotted all over the place in groups ... were dashing around. There were more of them than had ever been seen before. They were so confident that they had even brought their wives to see them win the battle and had stationed them in wagons parked at the edge of the battlefield ...

To begin the legions stood where they were, keeping to the narrow valley for protection. When the enemy came closer, they threw their javelins (spears) with accurate aim and then rushed forward in a wedge formation ... the cavalry with their spears at the ready broke down all who resisted them. The rest of the Britons fled, although it was not easy because the line of wagons blocked their way. The troops showed no mercy even to the women ... It was a glorious victory ... according to some accounts, a few less than 80 000 Britons perished (died). Boudica ended her life by taking poison.

Cornelius Tacitus, The Annals.

After the Battle

When he had defeated Boudica, Suetonius kept his army together and attacked all the tribes of the Britons who were not friendly towards the Romans. He burnt their villages and killed anyone who did not escape.

? *Why do you think the Romans succeeded in beating the Britons, even though they had a smaller army?*

CORE ACTIVITIES

1 Using the information in this unit:
  - Follow the movements of the Romans and Britons on the map (**H**).

2 CAUSATION is when people or events cause something else to happen. A chain of events caused Boudica to take action.
  - Design a flow chart to show these events. You could begin:
    - Event 1 - The death of Boudica's husband led to ——>
    - Event 2 - He left half his money to his daughters and half to the Emperor. This led to ——>
    - Event 3 - ... and so on until the death of Boudica.

3 Now write a short report explaining why you think Boudica decided to fight against the Romans.
  - Try to include as many reasons as possible from the information in this unit.

4 Read **J**.
  - Draw a plan to show the battle.
  - Use labels to show:
    - the army of Suetonius (his troops and cavalry)
    - the army of Boudica
  - Use coloured lines to show the movements of the Romans.

EXTENSION ACTIVITY

1 You are a Roman reporter travelling with Suetonius' army.
  - Using the evidence in this unit, write a newspaper report to send back to Rome. Remember to make it quite clear that you are on the side of the Romans.
  - Ask your teacher if you can write your report on a word processor.
  - Explain why Suetonius went to Anglesey.
  - Describe what Boudica and the Britons did at Colchester and London.
  - Describe what Boudica looked like.
  - Describe the final battle and the death of Boudica.
  - You could include drawings to illustrate your report.

9. WOMEN IN ROMAN TIMES

800 B.C.
700
600
500
400
300
200
100
0
100
200
300
400
500 A.D.

Targets

AT 3
* To interpret historical sources.
* To identify differences between the life of women in Roman times and today.

AT 1

Roman Women

Until the 20th century women could expect to die at a much younger age than men. This was mainly due to a life of hard work and giving birth to many children. Diseases such as plague and typhoid also meant that an early death was likely, although men also died from these diseases. A woman in Roman times was only likely to live until the age of 28 years. A man could expect to live to the age of 31 years. Of course, these are only average ages. Many people lived beyond these.

Education and Marriage

After a basic education, a girl would help in the home until the day of her marriage. Some girls were married at the age of 13 years. The marriage would be arranged by the girl's father, who would pay a dowry (an agreed amount of gold or silver) to her husband. The marriage was not finally agreed until the couple had lived together for a year.

If the wife was unhappy, she simply slept away from home for 3 nights each year and the marriage was not agreed. Divorce was quite common among wealthy Romans. However, there were many happy marriages.

A

B

Farewell, Lady Pantha from your husband. After your departure, I keep my lasting grief of your cruel death. Hera, goddess of marriage, never saw such a wife. Your beauty, your wisdom, your chastity ... You guided straight the rudder of life in our home and raised high our common fame in healing - though you were a woman you were not behind me in skill. In recognition of this, your bridegroom Glycon built this tomb for you.

An inscription from a tomb, 2nd century A.D.

? *Working with a friend, translate this source into modern-day language. What profession had Lady Pantha practised with her husband?*

A woman was expected to obey her husband. If he died, she was then under the control of her son or another male relative. Women who did not marry would usually live with a married brother or sister.

Male children were valued much more highly than daughters. Perhaps this was because they would become citizens and take part in public life. When a baby was born the father decided whether or not it would be allowed to live. Thousands of new-born baby girls were put on public refuse dumps to die. They were often eaten by dogs.

A model of a Roman woman spinning wool.
? *What do you think this woman's dress might be made from?*

Understanding and Evidence

A new-born baby being bathed by a midwife.

D

... as soon as we get paid our wages, I'll send them to you. If, as well may happen, you have a baby, let it live if it is a boy. But if it is a girl, expose it (put it out to die). Don't forget me. How can I forget you? I beg you then not to be anxious (worried).

An anonymous letter, written during Roman times, from a husband to his wife.

❓ *Who is making the decision about whether the baby lives or dies?*

Girls who were allowed to live would be under the care of their fathers and family. Once a girl married she was then under the control of her husband. A girl who did not marry usually had very little to do. On the death of her father she would usually live with a married brother, who would then become responsible for her.

After getting married a woman's main job was to cook and look after the house. She was also responsible for the spinning and weaving of cloth. Once children were born she had to look after them. Wealthy women had very few household tasks to do. These were done by slaves, who were under the control of the mistress of the house. If you look on to Unit 13, you will have an idea of the sort of house a wealthy Roman family might live in.

A wealthy Roman lady and her slaves, from a funeral monument made in Roman times. Poor women and slaves had to work both in the home and outside it.

❓ *What is happening in this picture?*

Wealthy women could spend time on their appearance. Both men and women curled their hair with tongs. They also put oil and grease on their hair to make it grow. Women used perfumed oil on their bodies and wore make-up and jewellery. Some women even wore wigs and false teeth.

An engraving showing a shop.

❓ *What are these women doing?*

Women were not allowed to be citizens, and during the Republic even wealthy women could not own property. However, from the time of Caesar women were allowed to own property. They also became less tied to the home and were allowed to go to circuses and other entertainments. (See Unit 17 for more information about entertainment.)

A reconstruction of a Roman tenement block. In Rome, poor people lived in blocks like this.

Women in Roman Britain

The Roman women who first came to Britain were the wives of commanders, and their slaves. One of the earliest examples of women's writing is from Vindolanda - a Roman fort in Northumberland. The writing is in Latin and is written in ink on a wafer-thin piece of birch tree bark.

H

Greetings Lepidina. Make sure that you come to my birthday celebration on the third day before the Ides of September. Wishing you good health. From your close friend Flavia Severa.

Flavia Severa, writing in about 100 A.D.

? *Who might Flavia Severa have been? What date in September was the 'Ides'? (CLUE TO SUCCESS: Look back at Unit 5)*

Women of the Ancient Britons

Although the women of the ancient Britons did not have such luxuries as baths and stone-built villas, the wealthy did have servants. The servants cared for the children and were responsible for the domestic arrangements in the home, just like the Roman women.

However, the women in ancient Britain seem to have had more freedom and independence than the Roman women. A wife was expected to take over the responsibilities of her husband on his death, and women were also allowed to fight in battle. **I** tells us about the involvement of women in the battle at Anglesey against Suetonius.

Understanding and Evidence

I

Women wove their way in and out of the battle lines. They looked just like Furies dressed in black robes, with their hair all loose, and brandishing torches ... The troops were dumb founded at this strange spectacle.

Cornelius Tacitus, The Annals.

J

She was more intelligent than women usually are.

Cornelius Tacitus, The Annals.

? Do you think the Roman troops were used to seeing women in battle? How do you know?

? What can you learn from this source about the view Tacitus had of women?

Although we do not have any written evidence, it seems that men approved of the involvement of women in the public life of the tribes. We know that Queen Cartimandua ruled the Brigante tribe with her husband Venutius, but that they disagreed about whether or not to support the Romans. Eventually she lost the battle with her husband and was rescued by the Romans. However, this does show that women of the Britons were prepared to fight for what they believed in and to make their views known in public.

CORE ACTIVITIES

1 Use the evidence in this unit to complete the following chart.

	True/false	Evidence
Women lived longer than men.		
Only men could become citizens.		
Men were better healers.		
Girl babies were preferred to boys.		
Some women were slaves.		
Women did not work in shops.		
Women did not write to each other.		
Both British and Roman women spun wool.		
British women did not fight in battle.		

2 Working with a friend, look at all the visual sources (pictures) in this unit.
  - Say what you can learn about the lives of women from each source.
  - You are now going to decide which of the visual sources you think is the most useful to someone learning about the Romans.
    - Make a list of **A, C, E, F** and **G**, starting with the one that you think would be the most useful.
    - Explain why you think each would be useful.

3 Compare the lives of Roman women with those of the women of ancient Britain.
  - Explain what you think are the main differences.

4 Now compare the lives of Roman women with the lives of women today.
  - Explain what you think are:
    - the main similarities
    - the main differences

EXTENSION ACTIVITY

1 Working in a small group, do a project on Women in Roman Times.
  - You should include written work and drawings. One section could be a diary written as if you were a girl in Roman times.
  - Using this unit and other sections in this book, collect evidence about:
    - the lives of girls
    - marriage
    - women in the home
    - women at work
    - women and education
    - clothing
    - hairstyles
    - jewellery
    - make-up
    - what men thought about women
    - women as slaves

27

10. HADRIAN'S WALL

Targets

800 B.C.
700
600
500
400
300
200
100
0
100
200
300
400
500 A.D.

* To suggest why Hadrian's Wall was built. AT1
* To examine the effects of the wall. AT1

From 117 to 138 A.D. Hadrian was Roman Emperor. He brought peace and prosperity to the Roman people and spent many years travelling throughout the Empire. He was one of the first emperors to spend any length of time in Britain, and he is remembered particularly for the wall which he ordered to be built in Northumberland.

FACT FILE

- Built 122 A.D. by Emperor Hadrian.
- 117 kilometres long.
- Stretched from one side of Britain to the other.
- About 5 metres high and 3 metres thick.
- Built from carefully cut stone, earth and timber.
- There were 16 forts.
- Each fort held between 500 and 1 000 soldiers.
- Every 1 500 metres there was a mile castle.
- Between each mile castle there was a signal tower.
- The wall was built by soldiers.

A

Western section of the wall was first built of turf and timber

Mile-castles and turrets continued down the coast

The road and these two forts were part of Trajan's earlier frontier.

Solway Firth · Carlisle · Vindolanda · Hexham · Corbridge · Newcastle · South Shields · Alston · Penrith · Durham

By sea · By land · By sea · By land

ᴗᴗᴗ Hadrian's wall
■ Forts
● Present day towns
— Roman roads
--- Probable Roman roads
➤ Supply routes

Forts on Hadrian's Wall
1 Wallsend
2 Newcastle
3 Benwell
4 Rudchester
5 Haltonchesters
6 Chesters
7 Carrawburgh
8 Housesteads
9 Great Chesters
10 Carvoran
11 Birdoswald
12 Castlesteads
13 Stanwix
14 Burgh-by-Sands
15 Drumburgh
16 Bowness

Each fort on the wall held between 500 and 1000 soldiers

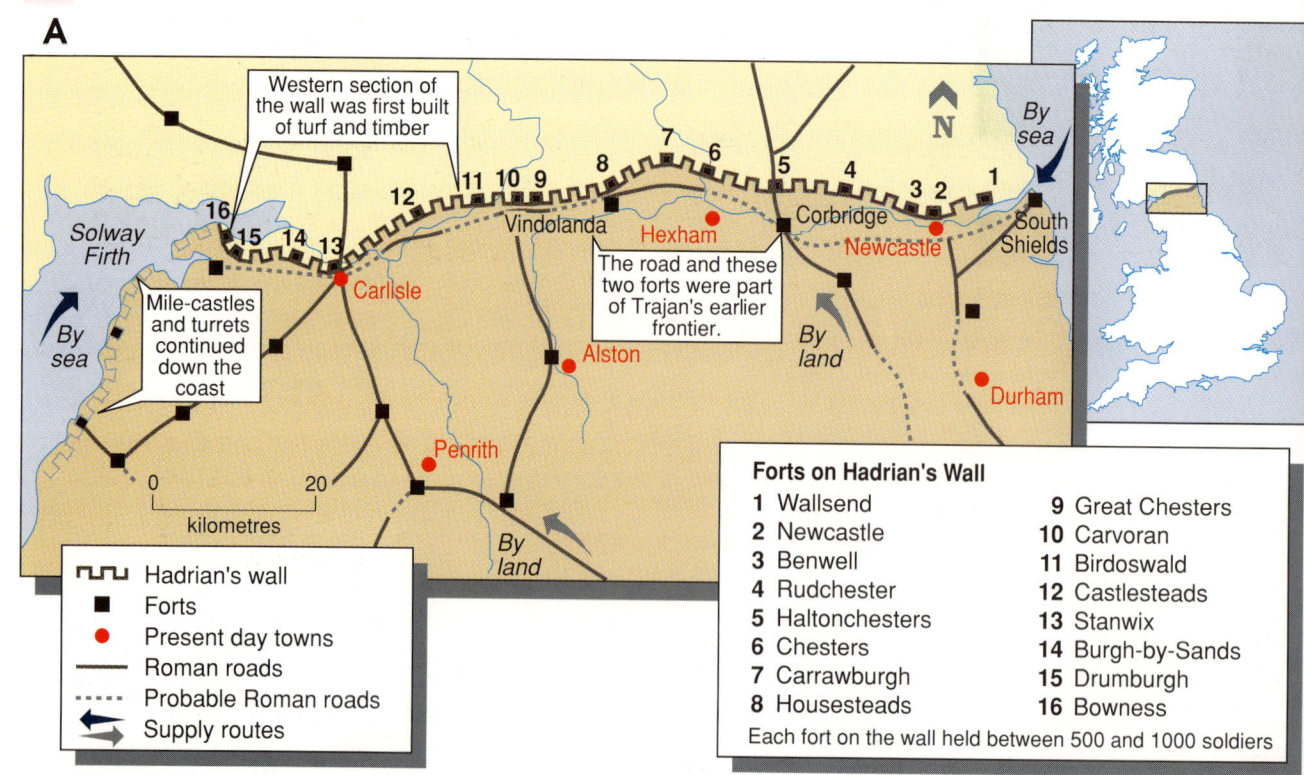

Map of Hadrian's Wall.

What Happened to the Wall?

At the beginning of Hadrian's rule the Empire had been expanding for nearly 900 years. Hadrian felt that it was getting too big to control. His policy was to strengthen the existing defences of the Empire and to stop the Empire growing further. Perhaps this is why he built the wall.

The Romans had trouble with the Britons to the north of the wall until 211 A.D., but this was followed by a century of peace. Roman soldiers living in the forts began to marry local women, and the sons of these

Understanding and Causation

couples also became Roman soldiers.

The wall attracted local people. Many small towns grew up beside the wall, together with markets and workshops. The army became part of the local community. Then, as the Roman Empire began to collapse, soldiers were gradually withdrawn from the wall to fight in other parts of the Empire. By 410 A.D. there were no regular Roman soldiers left in Britain at all.

B

When Hadrian became Emperor, those people whom Trajan had brought under control were breaking away from Rome ... The Britons could not be kept under Roman control ... he (Hadrian) went to Britain where he was the first to make a wall ... to separate the barbarians from the Romans.

Part of the Augustan History, written by an unknown author in about 380 A.D. Adapted from translation by A.R. Birley, Lives of the Later Caesars, 1976.

? What sorts of problem was Hadrian facing in Britain?

C

View of part of Hadrian's Wall today.

D

The same view as it might have looked in Roman times.

? How has the wall changed since Roman times?

CORE ACTIVITIES

1 You will need a large piece of paper.
  - On it make a careful copy of the Fact File.
  - Search through this unit and see if you can find evidence to support each fact. You could link each piece of evidence to the 'fact' by a line. Use drawings and writing to show the evidence you have used.

2 Discuss with some friends why you think the wall was built.
  - Now put the points below in order of importance. Begin with the one you think was the most important.
    - Hadrian wanted to stop expanding the Roman Empire.
    - Hadrian wanted to keep the Roman soldiers busy.
    - Hadrian wanted to stop the Britons from the north robbing the south.
    - Hadrian wanted to show the Britons that the Romans were in control.
    - Hadrian wanted to separate Roman Britain from the barbarians.
  - Explain why you have chosen your particular order for the points.
  - What effect do you think the wall might have had on people living in that area?

EXTENSION ACTIVITIES

1 The remains of Hadrian's Wall still exist today.
  - Ask your teacher if you can help plan a visit to the wall. *The English Tourist Board, 4 Grosvenor Gardens, London SW1W 0DU might be able to give further information.*

2 Using this unit and any other books which are available:
  - Find out more about Hadrian's Wall. You could prepare a short talk for the rest of the class or record a programme on a cassette.

29

11. A ROMAN FORT

800 B.C.
700
600
500
400
300
200
100
0
100
200
300
400
500 A.D.

Targets

* To use evidence to reconstruct the past. AT 1
* To put together information from different historical sources. AT 3

After the defeat of Boudica in 61 A.D. the Romans gradually overcame the tribes in Wales and northern Britain. Many Britons who did not wish to live under Roman rule fled to Scotland. The Roman army never succeeded in conquering all the people there.

As the Romans moved west and north they built roads and forts. One of these forts was at South Shields on the coast, to the west of Newcastle. Look back at **A** in Unit 10 and find South Shields.

The reconstructed west gate of the fort at South Shields.

? *Describe the windows. What do you think might have been the purpose of the shutter on each window?*

Why do you think the Romans built roads and forts? Why do you think the Romans chose to build a fort at South Shields?

The first fort at South Shields was probably built in about 78 A.D. and made out of wood. The Romans brought many of their supplies to the north by sea. These were landed at the port, then moved the short distance to the fort.

The supplies were used by the Roman soldiers who built Hadrian's Wall in about 122 A.D. In about 163 A.D. the fort at South Shields was rebuilt in stone.

Evidence

The West Gate

Perhaps you have visited some of the Roman forts on Hadrian's Wall in Northumberland. When you can only see ruins it is difficult to imagine how the fort might have looked in Roman times. At South Shields archaeologists have been able to reconstruct the west gate of the fort. It is built on the original Roman foundations, so the archaeologists were able to get the size exactly right. They also found one of the curved windowhead stones, so they were able to make copies of these.

Even though archaeologists used all the evidence they could find to make sure their reconstruction was accurate, people still say that they should not have built the gate. The argument they give is that the original Roman remains have been covered over by the gate. In other words, by reconstructing the gate the primary evidence has been spoilt.

During the 2nd century it is thought that 120 cavalry (soldiers on horseback) and 480 foot soldiers were stationed at South Shields fort. However, in 208 A.D. the Emperor, Septimus Severus, arrived in Britain and began trying to push further north into Scotland. Many of the buildings at the fort were demolished, and 20 huge granaries were built to store the supplies for Septimus Severus' army. The fort was also extended southwards.

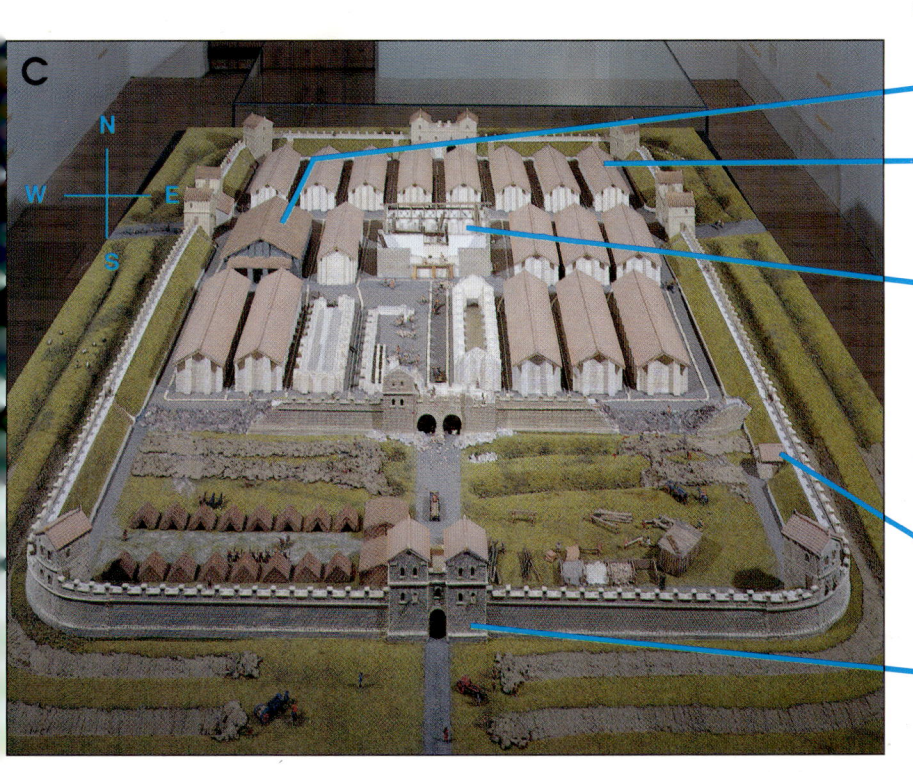

The west gate and other remains today.

? *Can you find the west gate on the model shown in C?*

LARGE HOUSE BUILT LATE IN 3rd CENTURY A.D.

GRANARIES 208 A.D.

HEADQUARTERS BUILDING. BUILT IN ABOUT 220 A.D.

A model of the fort as it might have looked in the 3rd century.

? *Can you spot where the fort has been extended to the south?*

LATRINE BUILT IN ABOUT 208 A.D.

SOUTH GATE 208 A.D.

D

A Roman soldier.

Soldiers in the Roman Army

The Romans were able to build up a big empire because of the size of their army. At its greatest strength the Roman army had over 500 000 men. These were divided into legions. Each legion had about 5 000 men, plus another 1 000 builders, engineers and craftsmen.

The legionary soldiers were the best soldiers. They were all Roman citizens who trained as professional soldiers and served in the army for 25 years. After that they were given a pension and a piece of land for a villa. (See Unit 13 for more information about villas.)

The auxiliaries, who also served for 25 years, were well-trained soldiers, but they were not Roman citizens. They were often awarded citizenship at the end of their service. Auxiliaries were often men who lived in countries which the Romans had conquered.

E

So a young soldier who is chosen ... should have alert eyes and should hold his head upright. The recruit should be broad-chested with powerful shoulders and brawny arms ... He should not be pot-bellied or have a fat bottom. His calves and feet should not be flabby; instead they should be made entirely of tough sinew (muscle). When you find these qualities in a recruit you can afford to take him even if he is a little on the short side. It is better for soldiers to be strong rather than tall.

Vegetius, a Roman official, writing in the 4th century A.D.

F

They equip them with round shields ... weighing twice as much as those used on the battlefield. They also give wooden swords double the weight of real ones. They are made to exercise in the afternoons as well as the mornings, using this equipment against a wooden post.

Vegetius, 4th century A.D.

? *Explain to a friend the sort of young soldier Vegetius was looking for. Why do you think he looked for young men with the features mentioned in E?*

? *Why do you think the training equipment was twice as heavy as that used on the battlefield?*

G

Roman soldiers building a fort.

H

They never stop training and they never wait for an emergency to arise ... Their exercises carried out in peacetime are just as hard-fought as the real thing. Every soldier puts all he has into his training, just as if he were taking part in a real war.

Flavius Josephus, The Jewish War, 1st century A.D.

? *Can you see anything in this relief which supports the suggestions of Vegetius in E?*

? *Why do you think training was considered so important?*

Evidence

I

Foot soldiers are armed with a cuirass (body armour) and a helmet. They carry two swords ... a spear and a round shield ... In addition ... a saw, a basket, a mattock (type of pick) and an axe, as well as a leather strap, a sickle, a chain and enough rations to last him for three days. In fact he carries so much equipment that he is not very different from a pack-mule.

Flavius Josephus, The Jewish War, 1st century A.D.

? About how much do you think all this equipment might weigh?

We do not have a great deal of evidence about what life was like in the forts on the northern border of the Roman Empire. However, some letters have been discovered on the site of the fort at Vindolanda. **J** is part of a letter written on a wafer-thin piece of tree bark. You can see the actual writing in the original Latin. **K** is the translation.

J

Fragment of a letter sent to a soldier at Vindolanda.

K

I have sent you ... pairs of socks from Sattua, two pairs of sandals and two pairs of underpants.

Translation of the letter fragment, written in about 100 A.D.

? What can you learn about the life of a soldier from this source?

CORE ACTIVITIES

1 Look back at the pages about the fort at South Shields. In particular, look at **A** and read about the reconstructed west gate.
- Decide whether or not you think the archaeologists should have reconstructed the gate on top of the Roman remains.
- Give reasons for your answer.
- Make a list of the evidence which the archaeologists might have used to decide what the gate looked like.
- Find another person and explain your answers to them.
- Listen to their answers and ask them questions about what they have decided.

2 Using the information and evidence in this unit:
- Write a guide book for visitors to the fort at South Shields.
- You should include:
  - a brief history of the fort
  - a map showing where the fort is on the wall (see **A** in Unit 10)
  - a plan of the fort (**C** will be helpful)
  - a labelled drawing of the west gate
  - a list of questions which visitors might ask when they visit the site
  - a short section about the life of soldiers who might have lived at the fort
- If you have access to a computer with a word processing program, you could print your guide book.

EXTENSION ACTIVITY

1 Look again at the evidence in this unit about the life of soldiers in the Roman army.
- Collect further evidence about the life of Roman soldiers.
- Using the evidence in this unit and the additional evidence you have collected, write a Soldier's Handbook.
- You should include writing and drawings to show:
  - how soldiers were selected
  - how they were trained
  - a sketch of a soldier and a list of his equipment
  - the type of work a soldier was expected to do
  - details about length of service and retirement
  - any other information which a soldier would need to know

12. TOWN AND COUNTRY LIFE

Targets

800 B.C.
700
600
500
400
300
200
100
0
100
200
300
400
500 A.D.

* To identify aspects of life which changed and aspects of life which did not change. AT 1
* To show how life in the town and countryside were related. AT 1

Town Life

The Romans built many towns in Britain. Sometimes these towns were built as army bases. Other towns, like Colchester, were built as colonies for retired soldiers. You will remember that it was Colchester that Boudica burnt to the ground in 61 A.D. The town of Colchester today is built on top of the Roman town of Colchester.

A

Colchester today.

? *Can you spot the main Roman streets in modern Colchester?*

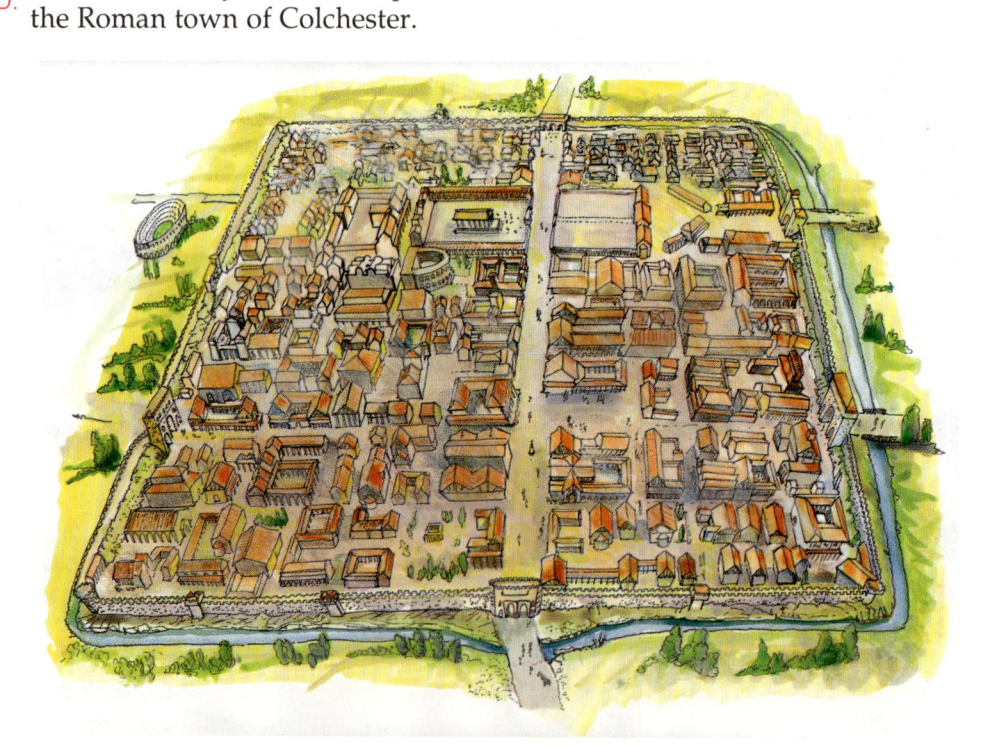

B

How Colchester might have looked in Roman times.

CORE ACTIVITIES

1 Before the Romans arrived, the Britons lived in huts with thatched roofs, clustered together in small isolated farming communities.
  ● Look at **B**, then make a list of the things which changed for Britons when the Romans came.

2 Now read the section on farming.
  ● Explain whether you think life on farms changed as much as life in towns during Roman times.
  ● Check out your answers with a friend.

Change

Country Life

Farming was the most important occupation for Romans, although the actual work was done by slaves or the very poor. Most wealthy Romans employed managers to look after their farms.

C

The farm manager must not be an idler ... He must be the first to rise in the morning and last to bed ... he must see that the farm is shut up and that everyone is asleep in the right place and that the animals have fodder.

Marcus Cato, a Roman writer.

? *What was the final duty of the day for the farm manager?*

The Importance of Animals

Animals provided almost every item for Roman life. Clothes were made from the wool of sheep. In Britain a waterproof cloak made from goat skin was very good for keeping out the rain. Shoes, buckles, bags and belts were made from leather, and so were animal harnesses and parts of the soldiers' armour. Animal fat was used for candles and bone for the handles of knives, as well as combs, hair pins, needles and dice. Wealthy people ate meat every day. The poor could not afford such meat and had to live on a diet of coarse dark-coloured bread and vegetables. Animals were also used for transport and sport.

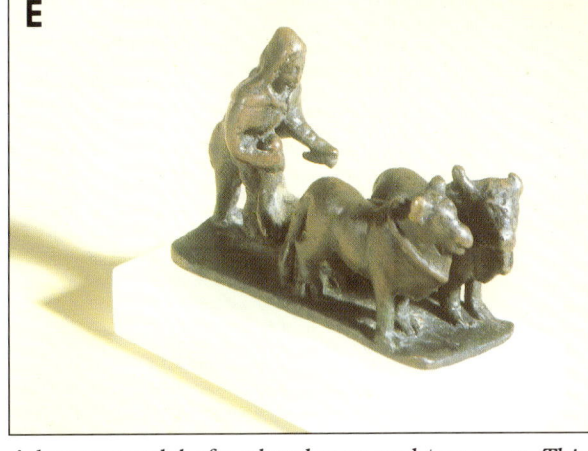

E

A bronze model of a ploughman and two oxen. This was found at Piercebridge in County Durham, although it was probably made in Gaul in about the 3rd century A.D.

D

Each slave in the chain gang should have 1.5 kilos of bread each day during the winter and 2 kilos when they begin work in the vineyard.

Marcus Cato, a Roman writer.

? *Why do you think the rations of a slave varied according to the work?*

Changes in Farming

Farmers in Britain used heavy ploughs pulled by oxen, like the one in E, before the Romans came. Although the Romans may have introduced a two-handled scythe for cutting corn, they brought very few changes to methods of farming.

However, the Romans did build roads and this made it much easier for farmers to transport their produce to market. More food was grown and taken to the growing number of towns in Roman Britain.

EXTENSION ACTIVITY

1 Imagine that you live in Roman Colchester.
   - Design a cartoon or write an account to show the activities which take place in the town.
   - Show how farming in the countryside around Colchester is linked to your life.
   (CLUE TO SUCCESS: Think about:
   - markets
   - food
   - wool
   - sports (Unit 17 will help))

13. A ROMAN VILLA

800 B.C.
700
600
500
400
300
200
100
0
100
200
300
400
500 A.D.

Targets

* To put together information from different sources. AT 3
* To compare the value of different sources. AT 3

As you will have seen from Unit 12, the Romans used the countryside for growing food. However, it was also the place where wealthy Romans built splendid houses. Some of the wealthy Britons also built villas and began to live in the Roman style. The remains of more than 100 villas have been found in Britain, and many more throughout Europe.

A Roman writer called Pliny owned several villas and often recommended life in the countryside to his friends.

The word 'villa' meant several different things to the Romans. It could mean a house in the country, a farmhouse, a farm or a farming estate.

A

Why not take the first opportunity to leave the noise, the senseless hullabaloo and useless effort of Rome and do some writing or just take a holiday.

A letter written by Pliny during the 1st century A.D.

? *Do any of Pliny's ideas seem similar to ours today?*

CORE ACTIVITIES

1 Using the sources and information in this unit:
- Prepare an estate agent's information sheet for Lullingstone villa.
- You should include:
  - a drawing of the villa labelled to show the building materials
  - a written description of the rooms with drawings to illustrate
  - details about the hypocaust system
  - information about the decoration
- You could try to draw a plan based on **B**.

B

A reconstruction of a Roman villa at Lullingstone in Kent. We do not have any written sources about Lullingstone, but Pliny did tell us about his villa.

2 In activity 1 you used a variety of historical evidence. Not all the evidence was about the villa at Lullingstone. Sometimes the only way to piece together a picture of the past is to use evidence from different places.
- Look at all the sources in this unit and decide which evidence was the most valuable when you did activity 1.
- You could list the sources in order of importance and explain the reasons for your choice.

Evidence

C

First you go into the atrium (entrance hall) ... from there into D-shaped colonnades enclosing a small but pleasant courtyard ... there is a rather nice dining room ... all around the dining room are folding doors or big windows ... from the back you can see the woods ... to the left of this ... is a large bedroom ... A bedroom on the other side ... has a raised floor and is fitted with pipes to receive hot steam and push it round at a set temperature ... the cooling room of the bathroom is large ... the two rest rooms ... lead to the heated swimming bath.

A letter from Pliny to his friend Gallus.

D

The atrium of a Roman villa in Pompeii.

? Can you identify any of the rooms mentioned by Pliny in the reconstructed villa shown in **B**?

E

A mosaic floor found at Lullingstone villa.

? How do you think mosaic floors were made?

Many villas had a pool in the atrium to collect rainwater from the open roof. Roman villas had very little furniture. The most common items were couches which were used in bedrooms, and extra large ones in the dining room. Sometimes as many as six people lay on one couch to eat their meal from a low table. The walls were beautifully decorated with frescos (paintings) and the floors were covered with mosaics.

Keeping Warm

One of the biggest problems in Roman Britain was keeping warm. The Romans had a form of central heating called hypocausts. **F** shows how the hot air from the fire was driven under the floor and up the walls of the room. Many villas also had private baths which were heated in the same way.

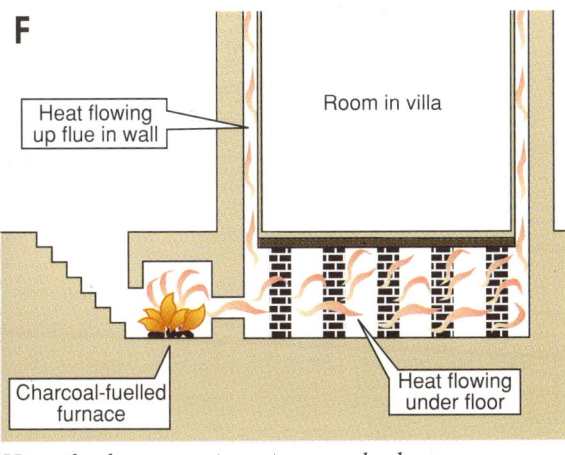

F

Heat flowing up flue in wall
Room in villa
Charcoal-fuelled furnace
Heat flowing under floor

How the hypocaust system worked.

? Who do you think was responsible for looking after the fire?

EXTENSION ACTIVITIES

1 Make a careful copy of **F**.
 • Label the following on your drawing:
  - the tiles which held up the floor
  - the space between the ground and the floor
  - the gaps in the walls

2 Can you find any evidence in **C** which suggests that Pliny had a hypocaust?
 • Collect and display more information about hypocausts.
 • What may have been the dangers of such heating systems?

14. ROMAN ENGINEERS

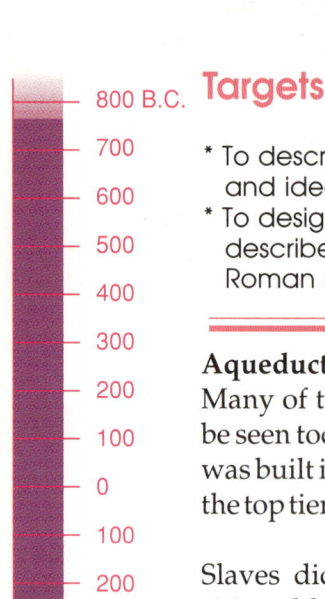

800 B.C.
700
600
500
400
300
200
100
0
100
200
300
400
500 A.D.

Targets

* To describe Roman attitudes and ideas about engineering.
* To design a poster which describes different forms of Roman engineering.

The Romans were skilled engineers. As well as villas and tenements they built large public buildings, roads, bridges, baths, toilets and aqueducts to carry water into their cities. They also constructed a system of sewers to take away human waste. These ran beneath their cities.

Aqueducts

Many of these feats of engineering can still be seen today. The Pont du Gard shown in **B** was built in 14 A.D. Water was carried along the top tier of arches 54 metres above ground.

Slaves did most of the building work in cities, although Roman soldiers often had to undertake military building projects. There were men who were trained as surveyors and engineers. Such men would be experienced in all kinds of construction work.

Building projects were usually organised by someone called a censor. Men called aediles were responsible for maintaining public works. Eventually they had men called Curator Aquarum (Director of Water Supplies) and Curator Viarum (Director of Roads).

A

My job concerns not merely the convenience, but also the health of the city ... The new Anio Aqueduct is taken from a river which is muddy ... Because of this a special filter tank was placed at the beginning of the aqueduct ... Six other aqueducts have filter tanks ... The aqueducts reach the city at different levels ... some deliver water to the higher ground and some to the lower ground. Compare such important engineering works carrying so much water with the idle pyramids and the useless though famous buildings of the Greeks.

Julius Frontinus, Water Commissioner for Rome, 97 A.D.

? How did the Romans solve the problem of muddy water?

Problems

Many problems had to be solved when building an aqueduct. The route had to be surveyed, slaves, craftsmen and building materials had to be found and the aqueduct had to slope in such a way that the water ran towards the city.

Roman Roads

The Romans relied on their armies to deal with any trouble in the Empire. So they needed good, straight roads along which soldiers could march quickly. Once the Romans had conquered a province they set about building roads. Most of the roads were built by soldiers.

B

Pont du Gard.

? Discuss with a partner how the Romans might have built this aqueduct. Remember that they did not have our modern machinery.

Evidence and Viewpoints

C

After restoring peace to his province, the Consul Flaminius would not allow soldiers to laze around and made them build a road from Bologna to Arretium.

Livy, a Roman historian who lived from 59 B.C. to 17 A.D.

? Give as many reasons as possible for the Consul making his men build this road.

Roman Roads in Britain

The Romans built their roads on a raised bank and also cut down all the trees and bushes which surrounded the road. Roads were mainly built in straight lines. When necessary, zigzags were used rather than bends. Roman roads were used by all kinds of travellers - soldiers, government officials, merchants and local farmers.

D

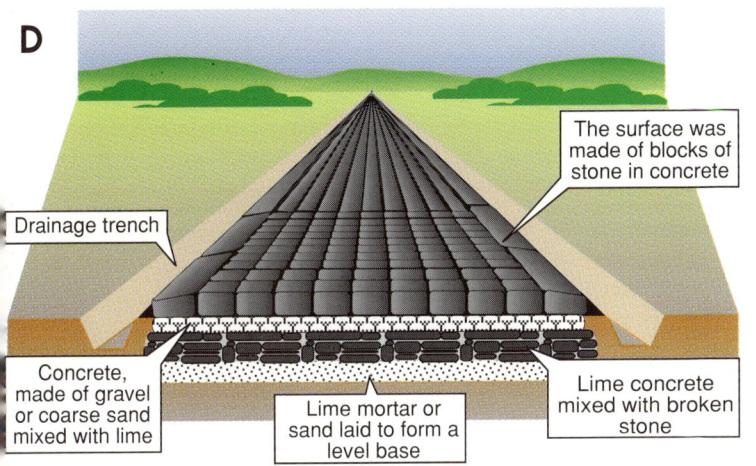

Drainage trench

The surface was made of blocks of stone in concrete

Concrete, made of gravel or coarse sand mixed with lime

Lime mortar or sand laid to form a level base

Lime concrete mixed with broken stone

Diagram of a Roman road.

? Why do you think the surface of the road is curved?

There were government rest houses along the main roads. Every road was measured and marked with Roman mile stones.

? Why do you think the Romans cleared the trees and bushes at the sides of the roads?

E

Map showing: Hadrian's Wall, York, Chester, Lincoln, Wroxeter, Leicester, Fosse Way, Ermine St, Cirencester, Watling Street, Colchester, Caerleon, St Albans, London, Bath, Silchester, Dover, Exeter, Chichester, English Channel, North Sea.

0 — 150 kilometres. N.

CORE ACTIVITIES

1 Read **A**.
- What does Julius Frontinus seem to think about Egyptian and Greek building compared to that of the Romans?

2 Read **A** and look carefully at **B**.
- If you were the censor organising the building of the Pont du Gard, list what you would need under the following headings: materials; craftsmen; the different skills they would need; equipment.

3 Think about the good ideas the Roman engineers had.
- Write a short account or design a comic strip showing some of them.

4 It is easy to build in a straight line if you can see the point you are trying to reach.
- How do you think the Romans built such long roads in a straight line? For example, look at Watling Street in **E**. How did the Romans make it so straight? *(CLUE TO SUCCESS*: Think about markers and bonfires*)*
- Check your answer with a partner.

EXTENSION ACTIVITY

1 Working in a small group:
- Design a poster to show all the different features of Roman engineering. *(CLUE TO SUCCESS*: Units 10, 15, 16, 17 and 21, and the information in this unit, will help)*
- Split your work up under the following headings: roads, aqueducts, bridges, public buildings, baths, toilets, houses.
- Use writing, labelled drawings and maps.
- Try to explain how the Romans actually built things and what tools they used.

39

15. MEDICINE AND PUBLIC HEALTH

Targets

* To show the difference between a fact and an opinion.
* To show that the sources we select can affect interpretation.

As you will have realised, the Romans were very practical people. They liked ideas and theories which could be put to very useful purposes. In early times they had no separate medical profession. They believed that every family had enough knowledge of herbs and medicines to treat themselves.

After 146 B.C., when part of Greece became a province of the Roman Empire, many Greek doctors came to Rome and Italy bringing their medical ideas with them. These Greek doctors were mainly used by the wealthy Romans.

A

White of egg can help to heal wounds. Yolk of egg boiled hard in vinegar and roasted with pepper stops diarrhoea. Nits can be removed with dog fat.

Pliny, Natural History, written in about 50 A.D.

? What is your opinion of these remedies?

B

'The Doctor'.

C

I will now give you some ideas about how the army can be kept healthy. Soldiers must not remain long near unhealthy marshes. A soldier who must face the cold without proper clothing is not in a state to have good health or to march. He must not drink swamp water. Daily exercise is better than the doctor for the soldiers. If a group of soldiers ... stay too long in one place ... they begin to suffer from the effects of polluted water, and are made miserable by the smell of their own excrement (waste). The air becomes unhealthy and they catch diseases.

Vegetius, a Roman writing in the 4th century A.D.

? What opinion does Vegetius seem to have of doctors?

D

Public toilets in a Roman town, North Africa.

? What are the main differences between these toilets and ours today?

The Army

Keeping the army healthy was essential if the Empire was to grow and to be kept in good order. You can tell from what Vegetius says that he was more concerned about preventing the soldiers becoming ill than he was about curing them! This was the beginning of Public Health, which really means that the state or government provides services to keep people healthy. In Rome and the provinces this meant the provision of fresh water for drinking and bathing, together with public toilets. It is thought that by 315 A.D. Rome had 144 public toilets, as well as toilets in the homes of the wealthy.

Evidence

Sewers

Both public and private toilets had good drainage systems or sewers to get rid of the waste.

E

Old men still admire the city sewers, the greatest achievement of all ... They were built 700 years ago ... and ... are still undamaged ... There are seven rivers made to flow in seven tunnels under the city. These finally run into one great sewer ... They sweep away all the sewage.

Pliny, Natural History.

F

Along your route each open window may be a death trap, so hope and pray, you poor man, that the local housewife drops nothing worse on your head than a bedpan full of slops.

Juvenal, Satires, written in about 100 A.D.

? *What was likely to land on the head of passers-by?*

Baths

The Romans probably took the idea of bathing from the Greeks, who realised how important personal cleanliness was for good health. The baths were built for the use of rich and poor people. The cost was one quadrans - about 1/16 of a penny today! Opening hours were usually from 1.00 p.m. until dusk. Both women and men used the baths, but they had to bath separately. By 326 A.D. there were 9 large baths in Rome. Some were big enough to hold 1 600 people and included shops, libraries, gardens and gym facilities.

The Great Bath at Bath.

H

In the heat of summer when your sweaty clothes stick to your body, a dive into the frigidarium (cold bath) wakes you right up ... In the cold of winter ... a dip in the calidarium (hot bath) makes you feel a new person.

Seneca, 4 B.C.-65 A.D.

CORE ACTIVITY

1 When studying historical sources we need to know whether the writer is giving us an opinion (what they think) or telling us a fact.
- Read the statements below and for each one say whether it is a fact or an opinion:
  - Daily exercise is better than the doctor for the soldiers (**C**).
  - ... the greatest achievement of all ... They were built 700 years ago (**E**).
  - ... a dip in the calidarium makes you feel a new person (**H**).
- Check your answers with a partner, and discuss your reasons.
- Most of the sources about the toilets, sewers and baths seem to suggest that Rome was a clean city. Can you find evidence in this unit to prove this was not true?

EXTENSION ACTIVITIES

1 Find out more about baths in Roman times.
- Look for information about baths at Roman forts, baths in private villas and baths in small towns.

2 Compare baths in Roman times with ours today.
- Draw two diagrams:
  - one to show how we use Roman ideas today
  - one to show the differences between Roman baths and ours

16. LIFE IN THE CITY OF ROME

800 B.C.
700
600
500
400
300
200
100
0
100
200
300
400
500 A.D.

Targets

* To write letters which demonstrate the fact that people's ideas and attitudes are related to their circumstances.
* To raise questions about pictorial evidence.

You already know a great deal about life in Rome. For example, you know from the story of Romulus and Remus how Rome began. You know about government and the law, and how public buildings, aqueducts, baths and toilets were built. In this unit you can learn a little more about the houses, shops and people of Rome. However, before reading any further, turn to Unit 17 in the Resource Book. There you will find a model of how historians think Rome looked in about 350 A.D. If you use the key, you will be able to find the buildings mentioned in this unit.

Shops and Houses

At the time of Romulus and Remus, Romans lived in round, thatched huts. Then better houses were built, until by the 2nd century B.C. rich Romans were building large houses. Poor Romans lived in blocks of flats which were small and crowded. These sometimes fell down owing to poor-quality building materials.

A

I hope you like my house. It was very small when I first bought it. I had some extra rooms built. It now has four dining rooms downstairs, twenty bedrooms, two marble porticoes (porches), a dining room upstairs, a bedroom where I sleep myself, a sitting room my wife uses and a room for the caretaker. I can have as many guests as a hotel.

From The Dinner of Trimalchio, a story written by the Roman writer Petronius in about 70 A.D.

? Even though this is a story, do you still think it is useful evidence?

B

A reconstruction of shops and houses in Rome. Notice the inner courtyards with gardens and pools. The open fronts are shops.

Viewpoints

Roman reliefs (carvings) showing shops. Can you identify which trade each shop is following?

The main shopping area was around the Forum, which was an open square. There was a great variety of shops including jewellers, butchers, florists, stone cutters, dressmakers, chemists, locksmiths, hairdressers and musical instrument makers. You could also hear speeches, watch the law courts and read public notices at the Forum.

Slavery

Without slaves it is doubtful whether the Romans could have built Rome. In fact there were probably 3 slaves for every Roman citizen. As foreign lands were defeated, thousands of slaves were shipped to Rome. We know that the Romans were always afraid that the slaves would rise up against them. Perhaps that is why slaves were beaten or put to death for quite small things.

Slaves who had special skills, such as doctors, teachers, musicians or craftsmen, were able to earn money. Later, during the Empire, they could buy their freedom or be freed on the death of their master. Some slaves lived comfortable lives in the homes of Roman citizens. Others were not so lucky!

CORE ACTIVITY

1 Using the information in this unit, you are going to write 2 letters as if you lived in Rome during the Empire. Each letter is to a friend.
- Letter 1.
  This is written as if you are a slave.
  - Try to describe the slave market and the house in which you live. You might work in your master's shop or have a special skill which you use in his household.
  - Explain if you are going to try to buy your freedom and how you feel about the Roman citizens.
- Letter 2.
  This is written as if you are a rich Roman like Trimalchio.
  - Describe your house, the slave market and how you feel towards the slaves.
  - Explain what happens in the Forum. Perhaps you could describe the funeral of a friend.
- You can illustrate your letters if you wish.
- Discuss with a partner why we find the Romans' attitude towards slaves difficult to understand.

EXTENSION ACTIVITIES

1 Look carefully at **C** and **D**.
- Then, working with a friend, make up one conversation which you think might be taking place in each picture.
- Make a list of the clues in **C** and **D** that you used.
- What have you learnt about the Romans from the pictures and your conversations?

2 What questions would you like to ask about what is happening in **C** and **D**?
- Try to research the answers to your questions.

17. LEISURE AND ENTERTAINMENT

Targets

* To say what can be learned from historical sources.
* To describe the attitudes of people in Roman times.

As so much work was done by slaves, Romans were left with a lot of leisure time. You have already learnt about the baths and the activities which happened there, but Romans also had many other ways of spending their leisure time. There was a great deal of public entertainment, for which large buildings were built. If you ask your teacher for Unit 17 from the Resource Book, you will be able to find the buildings mentioned in this unit.

The Colosseum today.
Look at the drawing of Rome in Unit 17 of the Resource Book and find this building.

Much of the public entertainment took place on festival days, which were holidays. There were 45 such days in each year. One of the most famous was the Lupercalia - 15th February - when young men ran around the old city wall hitting everyone they met with strips of goatskin! There was also the Saturnalia - 17th December - when presents were given and slaves could do as they pleased for that day.

The Colosseum

This massive amphitheatre was built in 80 A.D. for the games which the Romans enjoyed. These were held for a week in April and June, and a fortnight in September and November. The Colosseum could seat 60 000 people, yet it could be emptied in 3 or 4 minutes because there were 80 stairways and exits.

All the rock and marble for the Colosseum was cut to size where it was quarried. It was then transported to Rome where it was clamped into place with iron. There were many paintings on the walls, and statues of gods filled the hundreds of arches in the arena.

Entertainment at the Colosseum

Many events took place in this vast arena. Contests were fought between gladiators, and between gladiators and wild beasts. Sometimes animals were starved and then released into the arena to fight each other. Death by wild animals also became a punishment for criminals and slaves. As Christianity spread, many early Christians were killed in this way because they refused to worship Roman gods.

People could also watch firework displays and animal hunts, and on at least one occasion the arena was flooded for a mock sea battle. At the beginning of each day 7 eggs would be placed on a stand. These represented the 7 main events. After each event an egg would be removed.

Evidence

Gladiators

These men were slaves or prisoners who were trained at special schools to fight with great skill. Their rich owners would hire them out for public shows. Many died in their first fight, but a gladiator who survived several fights was often given his freedom. The Romans liked to see different types of gladiator fighting. For example, a popular fight would be between a retiarius, who wore no armour and fought with a net and a three-pronged fork, and a hoplomachi, a big man who fought in heavy armour. During the 1st century A.D. women gladiators also fought each other.

B

A gladiator and a bestiarius (animal fighter) in the arena.

? *What sort of animals are these men fighting? From which part of the Empire would these animals have come?*

C

He plunged his hunter's spear ... in a headlong-rushing bear, the king of beasts ... and he laid low a lion ... and with a far-dealt wound stretched in death a rushing pard (leopard). He won the prize of honour; yet unbroken still was his strength.

From Epigrams by a Roman poet called Martial, written in 80 A.D.

? *What does the poet seem to think of the gladiator?*

Seneca was visiting the amphitheatre during the midday break from the contests with animals. During this time criminals and slaves were forced to fight each other to the death. This is what Seneca means when he says they are thrown to the spectators. The last man alive was kept until the same time the next day.

D

I happened to call in at a midday show in the amphitheatre, expecting some sport, fun and relaxation. It was just the opposite. By comparison the fights that had already taken place were merciful. Now they really get down to business - it's sheer murder. In the morning men are thrown to the lions or bears; at noon they are thrown to the spectators.

Seneca, 1st century A.D.

? *What does Seneca's view of the 'sport' seem to be?*

E

He himself watched; he shouted ... and took away with him a mad passion which prodded him not only to return but even ... to drag in others.

St Augustine, writing about his friend Alypius in the 4th century A.D.

? *This was the first visit of Alypius to the Colosseum. Do you think he enjoyed the entertainment?*

45

F

A chariot race at the Circus Maximus.

How many horses seem to be pulling each chariot?

The Circus Maximus

This enormous arena was buil[t] for chariot racing. Up to 250 00[0] people could pack the Circus. Thi[s] was more like sport than the entertainment at the Colosseum but competitors were still ofte[n] killed.

The track was 600 metres long with rounded ends. Thes[e] rounded ends were the mos[t] dangerous. Chariots ofte[n] overturned as the drivers tried t[o] take them as quickly as possible. Usually 12 chariots raced 7 time[s] around the track. A driver wh[o] won could earn huge sums o[f] money. Diocles won 1 462 out o[f] 4 257 races and became a millionaire.

G

But it was the chariot-races that roused most excitement. Teams were the Reds, Whites, Greens and Blues and each had mobs of supporters. Hundreds of thousands in Rome queued up the night before the races. They betted heavily, rioted when their team won, and behaved like hooligans when it lost.

From a school textbook, The Ancient World. Published in 1974.

H

The Circus games do not interest me at all. If you've seen one race you've seen them all.

Pliny, a Roman writer, 1st century A.D.

I

A scene from the film Ben Hur.

Can you spot any evidence in **F** which suggests that it was used to reconstruct the scene in **I**?

Evidence

Theatres

There were several theatres in Rome, although these were not always as well attended as the Colosseum and Circus Maximus. Many of the Roman plays were copied from the Greeks. The performances were usually paid for by the magistrates, and the audience got in free. Large awnings or roofs protected the audience from the sun, and the air was often sprayed with perfume to keep people cool. Many of the actors wore masks. Costumes were of different colours for different characters so the audience could identify everyone. Theatres were built throughout the Empire.

Private Entertainment

Wealthy people entertained their friends to dinner in the evening. During the day people sat and talked. Evidence of board games - like our game of Ludo - has been found. We also know people played Knucklebones.

A reconstruction of a theatre at St Albans.
Can you spot the stage and the seats for the audience?

The actual site today.

CORE ACTIVITIES

1 Look carefully at all the written and visual sources.
   - Make a list of the primary sources and a list of the secondary sources.
   - Ask your teacher to explain the meaning of **PRIMARY** and **SECONDARY**.

2 Look carefully at **B**.
   - Describe it in detail to a partner. Note particularly the clothing and weapons.

3 What evidence is there in **B** which supports the information in the two sections called **The Colosseum** and **Entertainment at the Colosseum**?

4 Why do you think the people in **D** and **E** have such different views of the games?

5 What can you learn about Roman attitudes from **D**, **E**, **G** and **H**?

6 Make a copy of either **J** or **K**.
   - Label your drawing to show the stage, the seating and the orchestra (centre circle).
   - Are there any similarities with our theatres today?

EXTENSION ACTIVITY

1 Working in a small group, record a sports report which describes one of the following:
   - a day at the Colosseum
   - a chariot race at the Circus Maximus
   - a visit to the theatre
   - Try to describe it as if you were actually there. You may need to find out more about the topic you have chosen.
   - Ask your teacher if you can record your report on a cassette tape. Each group can then present their programme to the rest of the class.

47

18. THE FAMILY

800 B.C.
700
600
500
400
300
200
100
0
100
200
300
400
500 A.D.

Targets

* To identify differences between life today and life in Roman times.
* To write an illustrated booklet about a family living in ancient Rome.

The Roman Family

A Roman family was probably much larger than your family today. **A** gives you some idea of the people who might live within a Roman family. Of course, only wealthy Romans were able to afford slaves.

A

The extended Roman family.

The Father

The head of the household was the father. He had complete authority over all the other members of the household, and everyone had to obey his orders. He also held the power of life and death, particularly over slaves and new-born children.

Children

When a child was born the father decided whether it should be accepted into the family. It was very important to have a son in Roman times. Because of this many baby girls were put on rubbish dumps and left to die. The Romans probably thought it was important to have sons because only men played a part in public life and business. Sometimes a father who had 2 or 3 sons might give one away to a friend who had none of his own.

These actions may sound cruel to us today, but we do know that families enjoyed loving relationships. This is supported by the many tombstones which show the grief felt by a family when a loved one died.

C

To the Spirits of the departed and to Simplicia Florentina, a most innocent soul, who lived 10 months. Her father, Felicius Simplex, made this.

From a Roman tombstone.

B

A relief from Roman times showing a family

? *In what way does this evidence suggest that Simplicia was loved by her father?*

Change

Sons and Daughters

Once the baby had been accepted into the family by the father, offerings were made to the gods. A baby boy who was born into a high-class family was given a lucky charm called a bulla to wear around his neck. When he started to walk he was given a striped toga to wear. As soon as a boy needed to shave, his first beard hairs were put in a box and dedicated to the gods. This was a way of thanking the gods for letting the boy turn into a man. Once a boy reached 16 years, he was thought to be grown up and no longer wore his bulla or striped toga.

Girls were also given lucky charms. Marriages had usually been arranged for daughters by the age of 13 or 14. The night before her wedding a girl would put all her toys and lucky charms on the altar dedicated to the family god. This was a sign that the girl was now a woman.

D

Children at play.
What sort of games do these children seem to be playing?

Games

Children of the wealthy were educated and you can read more about this in Unit 19. However, children of the poor probably spent their time playing or begging for money from the wealthy. You can see two of the games they played in **D**. Children also played with wooden dolls, model soldiers, hoops and leather balls stuffed with hair or feathers. They also attended all the public entertainment enjoyed by their parents.

EXTENSION ACTIVITY

1 Using Units 9, 15, 16 and 17, write an illustrated booklet about life as a young person of your age in Roman times.
- You will need to collect quite a lot of information first and plan the headings for your pages. Unit 18 from the Resource Book will help.
- You could use the following headings:
  - the family
  - a new baby
  - my mother
  - my father
  - a visit to the baths
  - shopping in Rome
  - a visit to the circus
  - an evening meal with friends
- Perhaps your teacher will let you use a word processor to produce your booklet.

CORE ACTIVITIES

1 Talk with a friend about the differences between families and children today and those in Roman times.
- Then write a short account or make a drawing showing all the differences.

2 What can you learn about clothing in Roman times from the sources and information in this unit?

19. EDUCATION

Targets

* To use the information in this unit to answer questions.
* To put together information from this unit.

In Roman times children did not have to go to school like today. Education was not free and so only quite wealthy people were able to send their children to school. Also this was only possible if they lived near to a school. The Emperor Hadrian was eager for people to be better educated, so he offered special tax relief to teachers willing to start schools in the more remote areas.

A

People passing ... could hear the boys chanting their lessons ... Every now and then someone would get a good thrashing ... school was held between October and the end of June ... The teacher's pay was so low it was hardly worth mentioning. However, parents refused to pay the fees if their sons did not learn anything. To make sure they received their money some teachers pushed their students very hard. They breathed plenty of lamp smoke ... The cane was always ready, keeping the class in order.

An unknown Roman writer.

? *What do you think 'They breathed plenty of lamp smoke' might mean?*
(CLUE TO SUCCESS: The Romans used oil lamps to give light at night)

B

I	1	XI	11	XXX	30
II	2	XII	12	XL	40
III	3	XIII	13	L	50
IV	4	XIV	14	LX	60
V	5	XV	15	LXX	70
VI	6	XVI	16	LXXX	80
VII	7	XVII	17	XC	90
VIII	8	XVIII	18	C	100
IX	9	XIX	19	D	500
X	10	XX	20	M	1000

Elementary Education

Children began their education at the age of 7 years. Boys and girls went to separate schools, although fewer girls than boys were sent to school. Those girls who did go to school left at the age of 12 or 13 to learn skills in the home ready for marriage.

During their elementary education most children were taught reading, writing and arithmetic.

Watch out for the use of Roman numerals at the end of television programmes. Write the number down and then use **B** *to translate the Roman numerals into present-day numbers. You will then be able to find out when the programme was made.*

C

A lesson in school.
? *Try to describe the sort of books being used in* **C**.

Evidence

Secondary Education

Some children received lessons from the age of 12 to 15 years. The secondary school teachers, called grammarians, were better educated than the elementary school teachers. Education at this level cost almost 4 times as much as an elementary education. The young people were also taught different subjects. These were: history, music, geography, Latin and Greek. The boys were also taught how to speak well in public. It was important that the right teacher was chosen for a boy's secondary education.

D

It is most important for him to have the right tutor ... We must look for a tutor in Latin rhetoric (speaking) whose school shall combine a strict training along with good manners and, above all, strict morals.

Pliny writing to a friend in the 1st century AD.

? What sort of person does Pliny suggest should be found?

E

A music lesson.
? What instrument is being taught?

F

This is a wax tablet used by children for writing. A stylus (a pointed tool) was used to scratch letters into the soft wax.

CORE ACTIVITIES

1 When we are studying any period of history, we have to learn to ask questions. Below are some questions about education in Roman times.
- Use the information in this unit to answer the questions, but before doing that see if you can add to the list of questions.
- For each answer you should give supporting evidence from this unit.
  - Did all children go to school?
  - What subjects were taught in Roman schools?
  - What were the different stages of Roman education?
  - How did the teachers make sure their pupils behaved?
  - Other questions.

2 You are an inspector writing a report about your visits to Roman schools.
- Include information about the following:
  - The different levels of education: elementary, secondary, university.
  - The subjects that pupils were taught at the different levels.
  - The behaviour of the pupils.
  - Teachers - their pay, how they kept discipline, how they tried to make children learn.
  - Anything else you can learn from this unit.
- You could stand up in front of the class and explain your work as a Roman boy or girl would have to do.

University Education

Only a few young men went on to this level. They were taught about the problems of the time, together with history and the law. Students also had to collect information and then present it clearly in public. Most of these young men went on to a career in the law courts or government.

EXTENSION ACTIVITIES

1 Using **B**, try to do some simple adding sums using Roman numerals.

2 Find a partner and spend a few minutes discussing the differences between education in Roman times and education today.
- You could write a list of the differences.

20. RELIGION AND CHRISTIANITY

Targets

* To identify why people acted as they did.
* To recognise the results of an event.

During the period of the Roman Empire most people worshipped many gods. They believed that in order for things to go right they had to please the gods. The Romans thought that the best way to please the gods was to make sacrifices.

A

Before setting out for a war a Roman general would visit the temple of Jupiter ... There he would ask the gods' help, promising gifts if the war was successful.

Written in Roman times.

❓ *Why do you think the general promised gifts to the gods?*

The Gods

Jupiter was the king of the gods, and his wife Juno was the goddess of the sky. Vesta was the goddess of the hearth, and Mars the god of war. Venus, Minerva, Apollo, Vulcan, Diana and Janus were also gods, and there were many more. The gods were worshipped in their temples, but each household also had its own shrine where members of the household worshipped the gods every day. These shrines were rather like mini temples.

People conquered by the Romans were allowed to worship their own gods. However, after 27 B.C. everyone also had to worship the Emperor as a god.

B

Janus, the two-headed god. One head looked backwards and one looked forwards. Our month of January is named after this god.

C

A reconstruction of the temple at Colchester.

Mars, the god of war.

The goddess Juno.

❓ *Which of our months do you think is named after Juno?*

Causation and Motivation

D

A family shrine from a house in Pompeii.

❓ What similarities do you notice between **C** and **D**?

The Coming of Christianity

During the Roman period a new religion began to spread throughout the Empire. It was called Christianity. One of the main differences of this religion was that its followers believed in only one God.

F

And all went to enrol themselves, everyone to his own city. And Joseph also went up from Galilee, out of the city of Nazareth into Judaea, to the city of David, which is called Bethlehem, to enrol himself with Mary who was betrothed (engaged) to him, being great with child. And it came to pass, while they were there, the days were fulfilled that she should be delivered. And she brought forth her first-born son; and she wrapped him in swaddling clothes, and laid him in a manger, because there was no room for them in the inn.

Holy Bible, revised version: Luke, chapter 2, verses 3-7.

❓ Translate this source into your own words. Check with your teacher any words which you do not understand.

Sacrifices

When a sacrifice was made, people had to act in a proper way and say the right words, otherwise the sacrifice would be unlucky.

E

O gods, we make this sacrifice to you. May the citizens of Rome be blessed with good fortune in both war and peace. Keep safe the legions of Rome. Always guard the name of Rome and give our people health, safety and victory. Be honoured by the sacrifice of this animal (here the animal was killed) and be favourable to the Roman people.

Written in Roman times.

❓ Look at **K**. What sort of animals are about to be sacrificed?

G

A head of Christ from a Roman mosaic floor at Hinton St Mary, Dorset. Archaeologists know that this is a picture of Christ because the cross and the letter P behind his head were a secret sign of the Christians.

❓ How does this picture of Jesus Christ differ from the way he is often shown in pictures today?

53

The birth of Jesus marks the change from B.C. (**Before Christ**) to A.D. (**Anno Domini**, in the year of our Lord). However, Christ was probably born in about 4 B.C. When Jesus was about 30 years old, in 26 A.D. he began to preach. Large crowds gathered to listen to him. He preached that:
- there is only one God;
- you should love everyone, both friends and enemies;
- if you lead a good life you will live in heaven after your death; evil people will go to hell.

Jesus healed many people who were ill and gradually more and more people began to believe in the things he preached.

At this time Judaea, the country in which Jesus lived, was a province of the Roman Empire. The Romans were worried about the crowds who followed Jesus. The Jewish priests were also worried because Christ spoke against them and because he claimed to be the son of God and the leader of the Jews. The priests brought Jesus to the Roman governor and persuaded him that Christ should be put to death. He was crucified, but his followers believed that he came back from the dead. They travelled throughout the Roman Empire spreading the teachings of Jesus Christ.

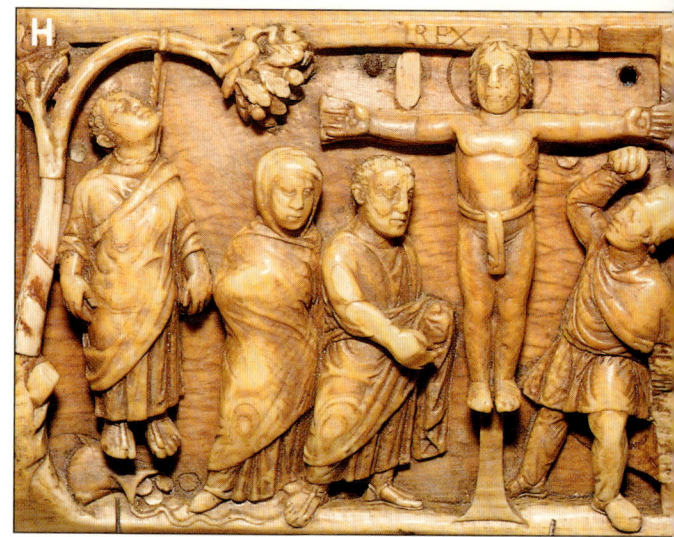

An ivory panel from about 420 A.D.
What scene is shown on this panel?
Who might be the figure hanging from the tree?

Romans and Christianity

You will remember that the Romans were quite happy for people to worship their own gods, as long as they worshipped the Emperor as well. However, because the Christians believed in only one God, they refused to worship the Emperor.

I

For the moment this is what I do to persons who might be Christians. I ask them if they are Christians, and if they admit it, I repeat the question a second and third time and warn them of the punishment that awaits them. If they persist (continue) I order them to be led away and executed.

A letter written by Gaius Pliny to Emperor Trajan in about 100 A.D.

J

These people must not be hunted out. If they are brought before you and they are guilty, they must be punished. But, in the case of anyone who denies he is a Christian and makes that clear by sacrifices to our gods, he is to be pardoned.

The reply of Emperor Trajan.

How could a Christian avoid being executed? Why do you think so many Christians refused to sacrifice to the gods?

Many Christians were punished for refusing to pray to the statue of the Emperor. Some were thrown into the arena to be killed by wild animals. Others were executed or sent to work in the mines. Many were tortured. Pliny, who wrote **I**, actually tortured men and women in order to find out more about Christianity and to get the names of those who were Christians.

Even though many Christians were put to death for their beliefs, Christianity still went on growing. It even spread to Britain, the most northerly part of the Roman Empire. Around 208 A.D., St Alban became the first Christian to be put to death in Britain.

Causation and Motivation

K

Emperor Constantine celebrating a victory by sacrificing animals to the gods.

? *This is a Roman relief from the time of Constantine. How do we know that he is shown as Emperor on this relief? (CLUE TO SUCCESS: Look at his head!)*

Emperor Constantine

In 306 A.D. Constantine was proclaimed Emperor in the city of York. However, he had many battles to fight before he was overall ruler of the Empire. His reign is important because he stopped the killing and torture of Christians and allowed them to worship their God, eventually becoming a Christian himself. We have no written evidence about how Constantine became a Christian. It seems that he might have had a vision or a dream on his journey to fight for Rome. After the battle, which he won, a law was passed in 313 A.D. allowing the Christians to worship, and returning any property which had been taken from them.

Constantine may have decided to stop the persecution of Christians because the number of people who worshipped Christ was growing and he needed support in his early days as Emperor. This may be the reason for Constantine not being baptised until a few hours before his death in 337 A.D.

Even though Christianity was the official religion of the Empire, people still worshipped pagan gods and continued with pagan customs and sacrifices.

CORE ACTIVITIES

Working with a friend, talk about your answers to the questions below. When you have discussed your answers, write them out in full sentences.

1 Why do you think the Romans first began to worship gods?

2 Write an account of the coming of Christianity, using dates to show the order of events.

3 Why do you think the Romans were worried about Christ?
  - Suggest as many reasons as possible.

4 Why do you think the Jewish priests persuaded the Romans to put Jesus Christ to death?

5 What evidence in this unit shows that the Romans disliked Christians?
  - Use quotations to support your answer.

6 Why do you think the Romans put so many Christians to death?

7 What do you think made Constantine become a Christian?

8 Even after Constantine became a Christian, **K** shows that he still made sacrifices to the gods.
  - Why do you think he did this?

EXTENSION ACTIVITIES

1 Look again at **B** and the section on Roman gods.
  - Using any books which are available to you, find out more about them.
  - You could present your findings in a booklet or on a large poster for display.

2 Using the information in this unit:
  - What do you think were the immediate (short-term) results for Roman people if they became Christian before 313 A.D.?
  - What have been the long-term results of Christ's teaching? *(CLUE TO SUCCESS: Question 2 is rather difficult. Don't worry, go and talk to your friends and your teacher about the answers)*

21. THE ARTS

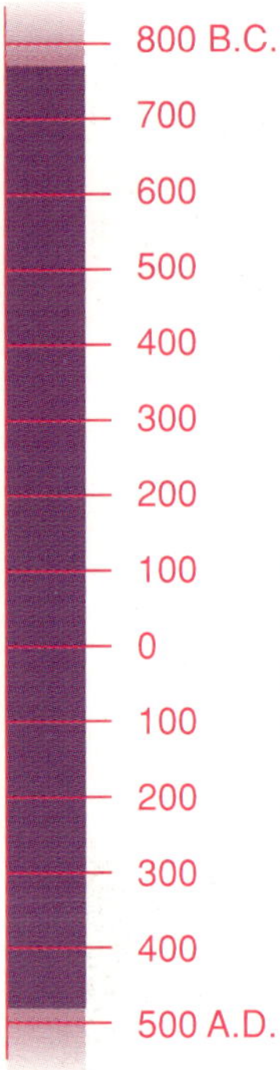

800 B.C.
700
600
500
400
300
200
100
0
100
200
300
400
500 A.D.

Targets

* To explain what you can learn from Roman art.
* To decide how useful Roman art is as historical evidence.

Painting and Sculpture

More than anything, the Romans wanted their paintings and sculptures to look like real people. Statues and paintings had to be realistic, with every hair and wart showing. Emperors and their families wanted to recognise themselves, and they wanted every detail to be accurate. This means that historians can learn a great deal about life in Roman times by studying the art which has survived.

Many of these works of art were completed by artists who were Greeks. This is because Greece was part of the Roman Empire, and Greek artists became slaves to the Romans.

Mosaic pictures were very popular with wealthy Romans. They used them for the floors of their villas and bath houses (see Unit 13). They were made up of small cubes of different coloured stone or glass set into plaster.

A

Since the days of the poet Pacuvius, the profession of painter has had no honour with the well born.

Pliny, writing in the 1st century A.D.

? Why do you think wealthy Romans did not learn to paint?

B

Marcus Aurelius in about 169 A.D.

? Can you find any other evidence in this unit to support the idea that this statue is a good likeness of Marcus Aurelius?

Relief work was also popular in Roman times. This was done by carving stone to make the figures stand out from a flat background. The Emperor Trajan wanted everyone to know how he had defeated the Dacians, who lived in the country we now call Romania. So he had a 40 metre high column erected in Rome, with a statue of himself on top. Winding all around the column was a series of scenes done in relief, rather like a modern-day comic strip. If you look back to **G** in Unit 5 you will find a scene from Trajan's Column.

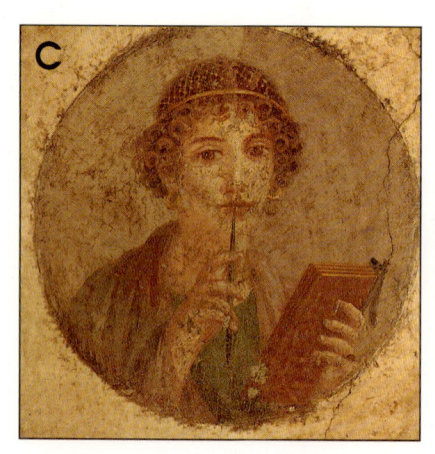

C

Portrait of a girl from Naples.
? What sort of person does this girl seem to be?

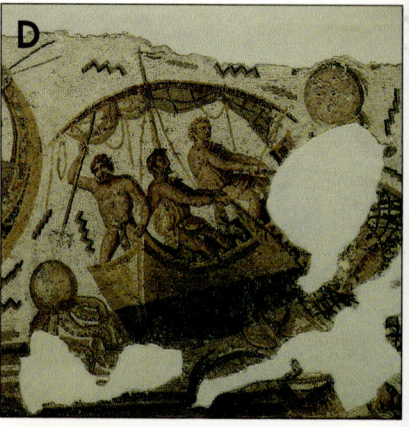

D

Mosaic from Thugga, 3rd century A.D.
? Discuss with a partner how a mosaic picture might be made.

Evidence

Architecture

You have already looked at several pieces of evidence in this book which show Roman buildings. For example, **E** in this unit shows buildings behind Marcus Aurelius. The style of these buildings is very much like that of the Greeks.

The Pantheon, built in 27 B.C.

Inside the dome of the Pantheon.

A relief showing Marcus Aurelius about to make a sacrifice, 2nd century A.D.

? What animal is Marcus Aurelius about to sacrifice?

The Romans used brick, tile and stone for their buildings. They also made concrete by mixing gravel, mortar and volcanic ash. This concrete was often poured into huge wooden moulds and left to set. In this way the Roman builders were able to make many different shapes, including domes like the one on the Pantheon.

The Pantheon

This was a Roman temple dedicated to many different gods. You will notice that the front looks like a Greek temple, but behind this is a huge round room. The room is 43 metres across and the roof is an enormous dome. The only window is a round hole in the centre of the dome. Although the dome was made 2 000 years ago, it is still standing today.

Music

Music was a very popular form of entertainment in Roman times. People sang both individually and in large choirs at religious festivals and the games. There were also many different types of instrument.

The tibia was the most widely used wind instrument. It was a pipe made from bronze, wood or ivory. Using their fingers, players covered the holes of the tibia to change the pitch. Often one musician would play two tibias at the same time.

The Arch of Constantine.

A relief from about 150 A.D. showing a young boy playing two tibias.

? *Describe to a partner how a tibia was played.*

A tuba was a long, straight trumpet. You can see one in **E**. A cornu was a large G-shaped instrument, which was wrapped around the head of the player and was often played in battle.

There were several different stringed instruments, such as the cithara. (If you look at **E** in Unit 19, you can see two boys learning to play the cithara.) This was made out of wood and usually had 5 to 7 strings. These strings were looped around bone pegs which could be turned for tuning. Other stringed instruments were the harp, which was mainly played by women, and the lute.

Percussion instruments such as cymbals, tambourines and wooden clappers were also played. These were popular because they were easy to play.

A relief from about 150 A.D. showing a battle scene.

? *Do you think this instrument is a trumpet or a cornu? Give reasons for your answer.*

Soloists travelled around the Empire playing the tibia and cithara. They were rather like our pop stars today, and were often mobbed by their fans!

Evidence

Literature

Much of our knowledge about the Romans comes from the words of their writers. The primary sources in this book are written by Roman writers.

Cicero (106-43 B.C.) wrote stories and speeches.
Caesar (102-44 B.C.) wrote manuals on the art of war.
Livy (59 B.C.-17 A.D.) wrote 142 books on the history of Rome.
Tacitus (55 A.D.-117 A.D.) wrote histories and biographies.
Plautus (c.251-184 B.C.) wrote 21 humorous and lively plays.
Terence (c.195-159 B.C.) also wrote plays.
Virgil (70-19 B.C.) was a poet whose greatest work was the Aeneid. This is a poem about a man called Aeneas who escapes from Troy and begins the great city of Rome.
Horace (65 B.C.-8 A.D.) was a poet who wrote about the good things of Roman history.
Ovid (43 B.C.-17 A.D.) was a poet who wrote fantastic tales. His poem Metamorphoses is about people who change shape.

K

The peasants were seized with a desire to plunge beneath the water ... Their voices became harsher ... their necks seemed to have disappeared ... their backs turned green and their bellies ... were white. So they were changed into frogs and, in their new shape, leaped about in the muddy pool.

Ovid's Metamorphoses, translated into prose by Mary Innes, 1955.

CORE ACTIVITIES

1. Look at **B**.
   - Describe the various pieces of riding equipment on this horse.
   - What can you learn about Roman horsemanship from this statue?

2. Look at **C**.
   - What can you learn from the painting about :
     - women's hairstyles?
     - headdresses?
     - education?

3. Look at **D**.
   - Explain to a partner what you can learn about Roman methods of fishing from the mosaic.

4. Look at **G**.
   - How do you think the Romans made the huge dome of the Pantheon?

5. Look at **I**.
   - What effect do you think the different-sized tibias would have had on the sound produced?

6. Using all the evidence about music in this unit:
   - Make a list of all the occasions when music was played or sung.
   - For each item on your list give supporting evidence.

7. Work with a partner and discuss whether or not you think Roman art is useful historical evidence.
   - Write your ideas down and discuss them with other people in your class.
   - Decide which form of Roman art is the most useful to a historian.

EXTENSION ACTIVITIES

1. Look again at the section on architecture.
   - Make some sketches of Roman buildings.
   - Take these sketches with you into your nearest town.
   - Take photographs or make sketches of any buildings which look similar to those of the Romans.

2. Using any other books available to you:
   - Find out more about Roman music.
   - Write up all your information in a project.
   - You could include:
     - drawings of instruments
     - explanations about how these instruments might have sounded
     - an advert for a concert given by a cithara player
   - Your music teacher might be able to help.

3. Find out more about any of the writers in the literature section.
   - You could write a short biography of your chosen writer.

22. COLLAPSE OF THE EMPIRE

Targets

* To place events in chronological order.
* To identify the reasons for the collapse of the Empire.

The Romans developed one of the largest, richest empires in the ancient world. As historians we must now ask ourselves why it came to an end. You can find some of the answers to that question in this unit. But you must remember that, as with most historical problems, there is no easy answer.

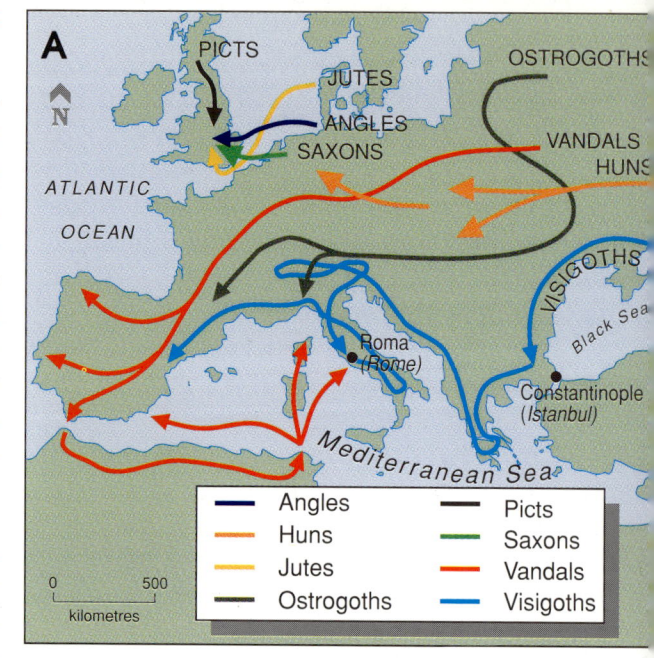

The Empire is Split

You will remember from Unit 20 that Emperor Constantine allowed Christians to worship freely, and that he eventually became a Christian himself. We know that the religion spread rapidly throughout the Empire. As Christianity is based on the idea that one should love one's enemies, it is possible that fewer Romans wished to fight to defend their Empire. However, we cannot be certain about this.

We do know that in 330 A.D. Constantine built a new city in the east, which was named Constantinople. This had the effect of splitting the Empire between two centres. By 395 A.D. there were two Roman Empires: one in the west with Rome as its capital, and one in the east with Constantinople as its capital.

A The barbarian attacks on the Empire.

? Why do you think the city in the east was called Constantinople?

Plague, Civil War and Barbarian Attacks

The Romans had always had a strong army. This was used to conquer other countries and also to defend the Empire against attacks from enemies. We know that from 200 A.D. Rome and the Empire suffered many epidemics of the plague. This was a dreadful disease which killed thousands of people. Many of these people were Roman soldiers.

We also know that leading Romans fought with each other to gain power and become Emperor. When people of the same nationality fight each other, it is called civil war. There were many civil wars in the Empire. These weakened the army, and the fierce tribes on the Roman borders took the opportunity to attack the Empire. **A** shows some of these tribes and their attacks. **B** shows what a Roman writer of the time wrote about one attack by the Huns in 395 A.D.

By 400 A.D. the Roman Emperor in the west was paying some of the barbarian tribes to fight on his side, and was letting them live inside the Empire. This was a bribe to stop the tribes attacking him.

B

Behold the wolves ... were let loose upon us ... and in a little while overran great provinces ... Many monasteries were captured ... many streams reddened with human blood! ... Flocks of captives were dragged away ... the whole east trembled, for swarms of Huns had broken forth from the far distance. They filled the whole earth with slaughter and panic ... on their swift horses ... The Roman army was away at the time and was detained in Italy owing to the civil wars.

Written by a Roman writer in 396 A.D.

? What can you learn about the Huns from this source?

Chronology and Causation

The Sack of Rome

The city of Rome had been defended from foreign invasion for over 800 years. But in August of 410 A.D. it was attacked by Alaric and his tribe of Visigoths. They slaughtered many of the Romans and took other citizens as slaves. Buildings were burnt and looted. The whole Roman Empire was shaken by the dreadful news.

In 455 A.D. Rome was attacked again by a tribe called the Vandals. The killing, robbing and looting went on for two weeks. By now many barbarian tribes were living in the Roman Empire. Finally, in 476 A.D., a Goth called Odoacer killed the last Roman Emperor in the west.

Roman Britain

Civil war and the attacks on the Empire had a disastrous effect on Roman Britain. From about 300 A.D. the Saxons from northern Germany had been attacking the east and south coasts. The Romans built forts along the coast to protect Britain. We know that the Picts from the north attacked 7 times in 340 A.D., and in 367 A.D. Picts, Scots and Saxons all attacked at the same time.

In 383 A.D. General Maximus abandoned Britain and took his army to Italy in an attempt to seize power and become Emperor. This left Britain open to further attacks. By 409 A.D. it seems unlikely that there were many Roman citizens left in Britain.

The End of the Empire

The city of Rome was eventually reduced to ruins. The law, trade and civilisation of the Romans gradually disappeared. The fierce tribes who had invaded the Empire continued to fight among themselves.

However, in the east the Empire around Constantinople continued to hold out against the barbarians and existed for a further 1 000 years. It became known as the Byzantine Empire. (You can learn more about the Byzantine Empire from Unit 22 in the Resource Book.)

> **C**
>
> 443 A.D. In this year the Britons sent overseas to Rome and asked them for troops against the Picts, but they had none there because they were at war with Attila, king of the Huns.
>
> *From the Laud Chronicle, written during the late 800s A.D.*

? What can we learn from this source about the plight of the Britons after the Romans had left?

D

A Saxon shore fort.

? Do you think the Romans thought the Saxons were a real danger? Give reasons for your answer.

CORE ACTIVITIES

1. Draw a time line and mark on it all the events described in this unit.
   - Your line should be 21 cm long, and each 7 cm should represent 100 years.
   - The line should begin in 200 A.D. and end in 500 A.D.

2. Working with a partner:
   - Make a list of all the reasons why you think the Roman Empire collapsed.
   - Now write out your list again, putting your reasons in order of importance.

EXTENSION ACTIVITIES

1. Draw a diagram or design a set of cartoons with captions to show the effect that the collapse of the Roman Empire had on:
   - Roman citizens
   - Britain

2. Look again at **C**.
   - Find out more about Attila the Hun, who died in 453 A.D.
   - You could write a short biography with illustrations to show some of the major events in his life.
   - Working with a partner, produce a television documentary about Attila's life.

23. THE LEGACY OF ROME

Target

* To identify ways in which the Romans still affect our lives today.

CORE ACTIVITY

1 Although it is more than 1 500 years since the collapse of the Roman Empire, there are still many ways in which the Romans affect our lives today.
- Before reading this unit, find a partner.
- Look back through this book and make a list of any Roman ideas or activities which are still used today. *(CLUE TO SUCCESS: You could either look through the book together or agree that each of you will look at certain units)*
- Now compare your list with the ideas in this unit.

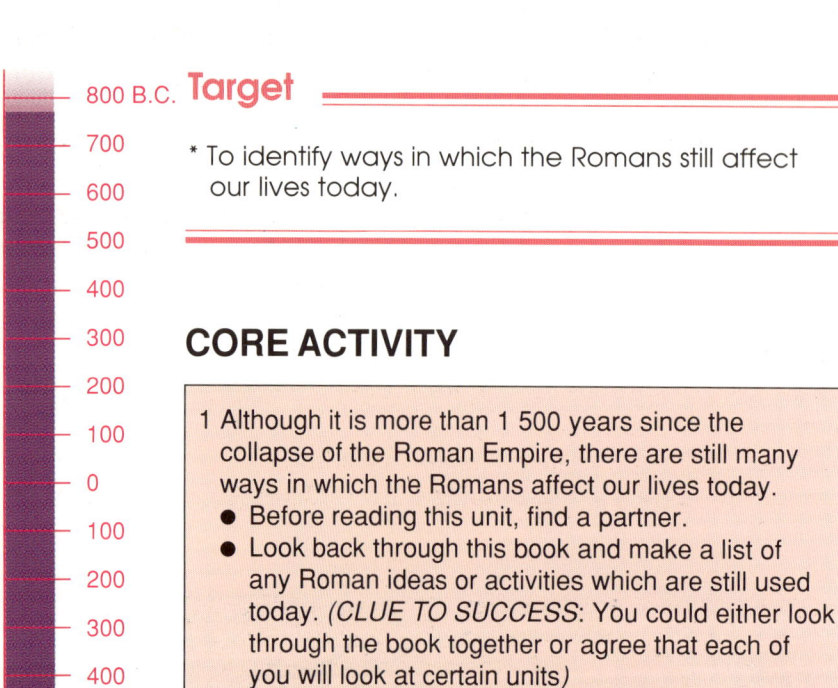

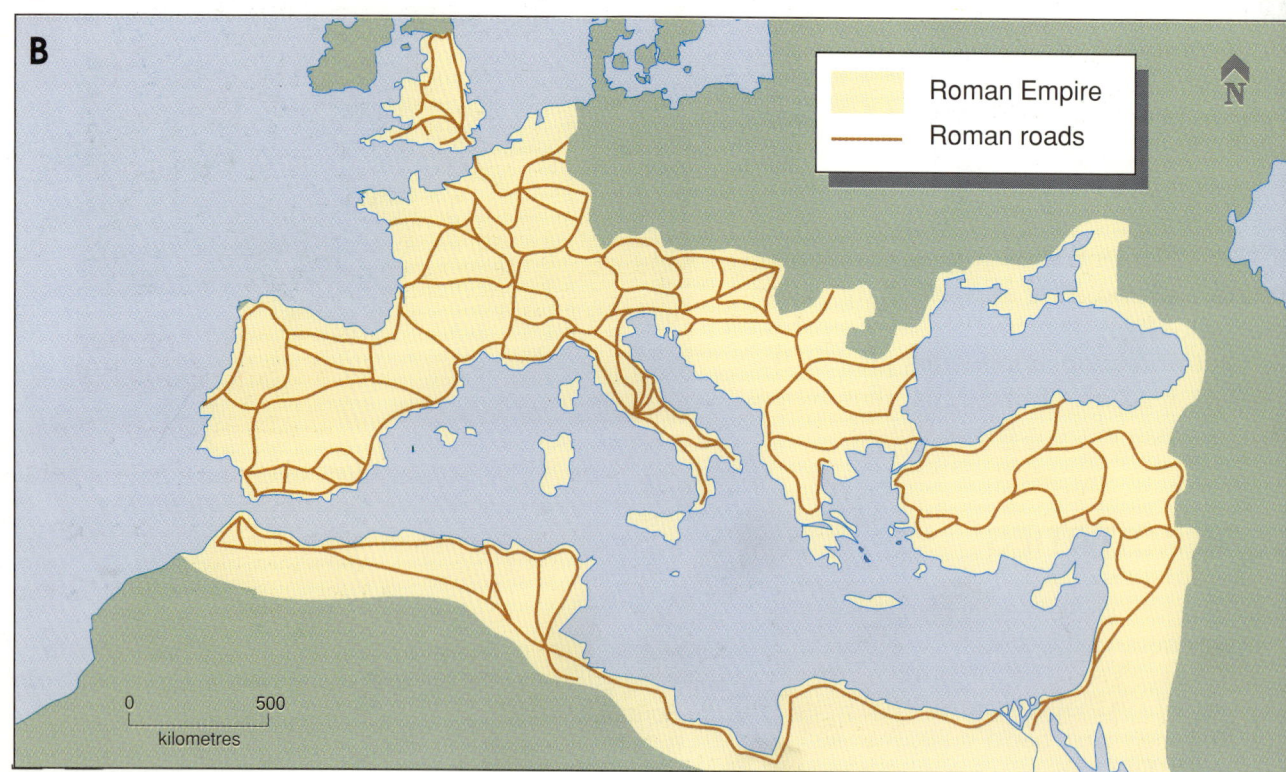

The roads of the Roman Empire.

The Roman Empire
- ▼ Communication by means of a network of roads (see **B**).
- ▼ The measurement of distance (see **C**).
- ▼ A public postal system. This was introduced by Emperor Hadrian.
- ▼ A calendar of 12 months. The names of our months today come from the Roman names.

Continuity

- The use of sundials, water clocks and hour glasses for telling the time (see **D**).
- The Latin language. This continued to be used by all educated people for over a thousand years after the collapse of the Empire. It is the basis of Spanish, Italian, French and Portuguese today. About one-third of English words also come from Latin.
- Architecture. Throughout the world you will find architecture which copies the ideas of the Romans (see **E**). We have also copied the use of bricks, cement and glass windows.
- Flats and central heating. The Romans were the first to build blocks of flats and install central heating systems.
- Towns planned according to a grid. Many towns today are built in the same way.
- The law. Rome's system of law and justice form the basis of Western law today, although the British system developed from Saxon ideas.
- A central government (in the Roman case, to administer a large empire).
- A banking system and coins (see **F**).
- The family. This was an important social unit in Roman times as it is today.
- The idea of preventing disease through the provision of public health facilities, e.g. fresh water, sewers, toilets and baths.

A Roman milestone.

The Roman temple at Nimes.

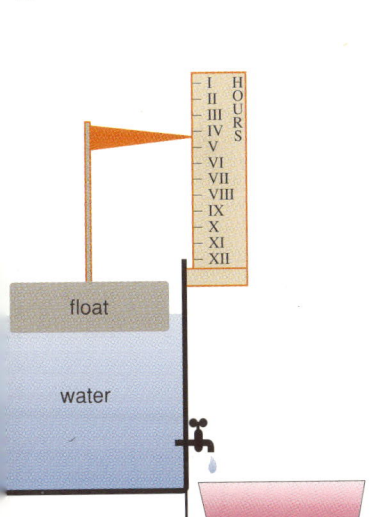

A Roman water clock.

A Roman coin of Septimus Severus.

EXTENSION ACTIVITY

1 Working with all the other people in your class:
   - Design a series of drawings to make into a frieze.
   - Each drawing should show one Roman idea which has influenced us today.
   - Beside each drawing you could add a photograph from a newspaper or magazine to show the modern-day equivalent. *(CLUE TO SUCCESS*: A drawing of a Roman bath with a photograph of a modern leisure centre)

INDEX

A

Anthony, Mark	16, 17
Augustus (Caesar Octavian)	16, 17
Aurelius, Marcus	56, 57

B

Baths	41
Boudica	20 -23, 30, 34
Brutus	16

C

Caesar, Julius	12, 13, 16, 18, 20, 59
Caesar, Octavian (Augustus)	16
Calendar	15, 62
Cato, Marcus	35
Cassius	16
Cassius, Dio	18, 22, 23
Cartimandua	27
Chariot Racing	46
Children	24 - 27, 48 - 49, 50 - 51
Cicero	9, 11, 59
Claudius	18, 19, 21
Cleopatra	17
Colosseum	44
Constantine	55, 58, 60

D

Druids	20, 21

E

Education	24, 50 - 51
Etruscans	4

G

Gladiators	44 - 45
Gods	52

H

Hadrian	28, 29, 50, 62
Hannibal	6, 7
Heating	37
Hera	24

J

Jesus Christ	53 - 54

L

Lepidus	16
Literature	59

M

Mars, the god of war	5, 52
Music	58

N

Nero	21

O

Ovid	59

P

Paulinus, Suetonius	16, 20 -23, 26
Pliny	36 - 37, 40 - 41, 46, 51, 54, 56
Pompey	12, 14
Public Libraries	15
Punishments	11

R

Roads	38 - 39, 62
Rome	4 - 5, 8, 15, 42 - 43, 61
Romulus and Remus	5, 42

S

Seneca	41, 45
Severus, Septimus	31
Slaves	25, 35, 38, 43, 45, 48
Socrates	9
Soldiers	13 - 14, 19, 22 - 23, 29 - 33, 60
Strabo	9

T

Tacitus, Cornelius	20 -23, 27, 59
Theatre	47
Trajan	29, 54, 56

V

Vegetius	32, 40
Vindolanda	26, 33

W

Women	24 - 27, 45, 48 - 49